Being

A JOURNEY

Pankaj Gupta

MANJUL
Manjul Publishing House

First published in India by

MANJUL

Manjul Publishing House
•C-16, Sector 3, Noida, Uttar Pradesh 201301 – India
Website: www.manjulindia.com

Registered Office:
• 10, Nishat Colony, Bhopal 462 003 – India

Distribution Centres
Ahmedabad, Bengaluru, Bhopal, Kolkata, Chennai,
Hyderabad, Mumbai, New Delhi, Pune

Being - A Journey

This edition first published in 2023

ISBN 978-93-5543-464-7

Printed and bound in India by Nutech Print Services-India

Blessings always
Guruji

DEDICATION

'We are all part of this Universe, and our spiritual growth is as important to me as any other aspect of life. I was introduced to Guru Ji Bade Mandir by my beloved wife, and during my first visit, I experienced a connection that defies verbal explanation. Since that moment, I have continually felt Guru Ji's presence by my side, and I have encountered numerous instances where I have received his blessings and guidance to navigate the vast ocean of life, the Maha Sagar.

It is with profound gratitude and reverence that I dedicate this book to Guru Ji, whose divine presence has illuminated my path and enriched my journey of self-discovery and spiritual awakening.'

Contents

Introduction | 7

Chapter 1
Introspection: The Current State of Awareness | 19

Chapter 2
Acknowledging Own Values | 37

Chapter 3
Communication: How to Communicate | 51

Chapter 4
Organising Time to Find Time | 69

Chapter 5
The Personal Growth Plan | 85

Chapter 6
Declutter | 101

Chapter 7
Business Plan or Career Plan | 111

Chapter 8
Your Mission and Vision | 125

Chapter 9
The Growth Environment | 139

Chapter 10
Focus and Accountability | 155

INTRODUCTION

Dear readers,

Thank you for embarking on this transformative journey of self-discovery through my humble book. I'm not a writer, but I want to share my authentic journey of self-understanding over the years. As an ordinary person, I had fulfilled my responsibilities, experienced highs and lows, and explored different jobs and business ventures. Through it all, I learned valuable lessons worth sharing. I continued to learn from fellow Business Network International (BNI) members, through workshops, books, and courses like Neurolinguistic Programming, Braining and Co-active Coaching. My thirst for knowledge led me to pursue certification courses in leadership from John Maxwell Academy. I joined BNI in 2013, and now, after years of joyful, passionate, and learning-filled experiences, I own a BNI franchise in Deira Dubai.

I vividly remember my friend Karan urging me to attend a BNI chapter meeting back in 2013. Curiosity led me to that room filled with enthusiastic business people eager to support one another through referrals. I realised the potential for business growth, and I promptly became a member. Little did I know where this journey was about to take me. Initially, my vision was limited to business opportunities.

While encountering thousands of members, I gleaned invaluable insights from their life experiences, my treasured golden nuggets. One lesson that stuck with me forever was the power of forward-thinking, always asking, 'What is next?' This mindset and the encouragement of fellow members and friends led me to write this book. It is my way of sharing my knowledge for the greater benefit of society and to help others transform their lives.

This book presents my learnings in a structured manner and is divided into ten workshops that can align individuals or teams with their true purpose.

But before you dive into these workshops, I invite you to reflect on these questions from chapter 1: Introspection. Explore what you currently do but don't want to, and what you want to do but haven't pursued.

Subsequent chapters delve into topics such as values and purpose, communication, time management, personal growth, decluttering, career planning, mission and vision, creating a growth environment, and accountability. Each chapter poses relevant questions to help you on your path of self-discovery and growth.

These questions have arisen during my own journey,

profoundly impacting my life. Join me in discovering a new version of yourself. During the journey, if you ever feel lost, don't hesitate to connect with me. Together, let's embark on this journey of transformation.

Warm regards,

Pankaj Gupta

www.pankajgupta.me

How about we start our journey by answering these questions?

1. What are some of the activities you find yourself currently engaged in, but you would rather not be doing?

2. What is something you have a strong desire to pursue, but haven't taken action on it yet?

3. How familiar are you with your non-negotiable values, and do you know effective ways to discover and define your values?

____

____

____

____

4. Have you contemplated the purpose of your life and what it means to you?

____

____

____

____

5. What patterns do you notice while you are engaged in self-talk and inner dialogue?

____

____

____

____

6. Are people accurately perceiving the message you intend to convey? Why or why not?

7. How often do you set aside dedicated quality time to spend with your family?

8. When was the last time you postponed something you wished to do due to lack of time? How would you feel if you have time to complete that activity?

9. Do you have a personal growth plan, and how does it differ from your career growth plan?

10. What steps are you taking to ensure the relevance of your relationships not just in the present, but also ten years from now?

11. When was the last time you organised your wardrobe? How did you determine what to discard and what to keep?

12. What are your past experiences that currently hinder your personal growth?

____

____

____

____

13. What strategies do you have in place to advance your career over the next 12 months?

____

____

____

____

14. Are you familiar with the GROW strategy? If yes, how can it support your personal and professional development?

____

____

____

____

15. Envision yourself five years from now. What actions are you taking to reach that future state?

16. How do you plan to align your team with your mission?

17. What is the prevailing environment within your organisation? How does it impact your work and the work of others?

18. Does your team feel comfortable taking risks? How do you handle failures and setbacks within your team?

19. How do you personally ensure accountability for your actions and goals?

20. When was the last time you assessed whether your current actions and behaviours align with your desired goals and aspirations?

Chapter 1

Introspection: The Current State of Awareness

'In the year 2003, everything around me was taking a toll. I decided to get up early and look into the eyes of the rising Sun.'

I would have loved to start my book with such a beautiful line. Nevertheless, I am starting with Milan, a gentleman in his early 40s belonging to the ten per cent of the world's population who had everything that was still a dream for the rest of the ninety per cent of the world.

Milan was the head of cyber security at one of the reputed property development firms in Dubai. He had an understanding and hard-working wife and two beautiful kids. The family lived in a four-BHK flat facing the Arabian sea in Dubai. Still, something was missing. Deep inside Milan was lost, feeling hollow.

Milan loved to sit on the window ledge of his bedroom and stare at the rising waves. However, today, the mesmerising view meant nothing to him. Instead, he found himself trapped in a loop of questioning his existence. Why, how, and where to, what for had been running through his mind for months.

'I guess you need coffee.'

Milan looked behind and found his wife Shalini holding two mugs of hot coffee. 'Vent,' she added.

Milan always felt lucky having Shalini as his life partner who was not only caring but also had all the patience in the world to give you that lending ear you always wanted. She was the best listener. Milan thought not to bother Shalini. But just after a few sips of his coffee decided to go with the flow and let it all out.

'Have you ever found yourself stuck in life, questioning your purpose of living? Every day I get up, go for a morning walk, get ready, drop my kids at school, go to work, rush home, and have dinner with you and the kids, and then sleep. Then, the next day I get up and do it all again. I love you and the kids. I love my job, but I have had this empty feeling in my stomach.'

His wife looked into his eyes placed her palms on his cheeks, smiled, and said, 'Congratulations. You are on your way to unleashing the superpower within you. It's called Introspection.'

Milan was usually flattered by his wife's smile, but today he needed clarification.

'I thought you would be worried that your husband is losing his mind,' he expressed his concern.

There was a pain in his voice as if the person he trusted the most and to whom he had openly discussed his thoughts did not understand him.

'Should I worry about this? Your outlook on life is changing for the better. You are asking yourself important questions that will change your perspective of looking at and facing life's challenges. You are on the journey of self-awareness. Should I feel sorry for you?' she answered, still smiling.

'And what on earth does introspection mean?' he asked for which Shalini answered as follows:

'Introspection is questioning your thoughts and actions. It is the first step towards knowing yourself better, getting a clear sense of purpose, and building strong relationships. Examine your internal feelings and reflect on their meaning.

'Introspection focuses your mind and allows you to develop and grow. In addition, it enhances your ability to understand your motivation and helps you escape the distractions of a fast-paced life.'

'How do you know about introspection?' Milan questioned his wife.

'Because recently I visited an information session for a core group of BNI, where this gentleman by the name of Pankaj Gupta was sharing knowledge and it just stuck to my mind,' she answered.

'Oh! You speaking about some kind of a coach?'

'No, not exactly. He is just like us who has been through various learning processes and now loves to share what he has learned. Now I have to go and get our girls ready for school. You too, get ready,' she replied.

She was about to leave the room when suddenly she stopped, looked back, and suggested, 'I have an idea. I have his contact details. Why don't you connect with him and see if he can assist you in understanding Introspection?'

Milan was a bit hesitant to contact a stranger directly and ask for something. He thought why not send a WhatsApp message and see if he got a response? In the message, Milan shared the conflict of thoughts within him and his conversation with his wife and asked me to be a guide in his new journey.

Our thinking creates our personality. But when we question our review, a war breaks out within us. We get restless and feel trapped in ourselves, as happened to Milan. So many of you can relate to his state of mind. I often receive emails from people asking me for ways to calm down their inner quests and help them find the answers. Therefore, I am reaching out to you all through my book, sharing the process which can be your guide whenever you need it.

Importance of Introspection in Self-Growth

I told all of you about Milan's message so that you could evaluate your thought process. Despite everything Milan had, he was not satisfied because, like him, most of us have moulded our lives. We all have different personalities, yet we have prepared our definition of success based on others' philosophies.

I always say, 'Success is defined by others, and happiness by us. You choose if you want to be happy or successful.'

We cannot become successful by seeing someone else's image in the mirror of our minds. We must understand that the journey of all of us are different. We must ask ourselves whether what we are struggling to achieve is truly what we need.

We cannot know ourselves until we question ourselves. Introspection helps you to steer and acknowledge your strengths. It allows you to know your feelings and manage your emotions. It benefits you in every area of life.

Knowing yourself is the key to success. The more you

understand yourself, the more you develop self-acceptance and happiness. Finally, being happy is paramount, isn't it?

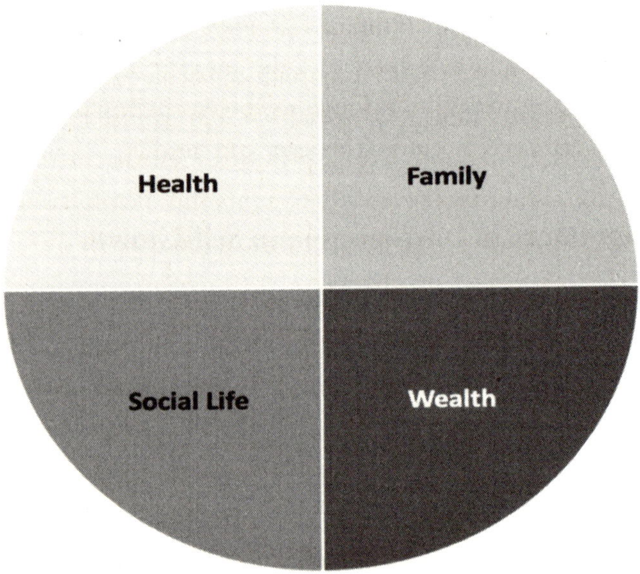

Introspection focuses on our interior life and helps in constructing ideas about who we are. Nevertheless, one significant issue is learning how to use introspection to improve our lives. People need to be aware of their actions and feelings. Looking inward and reflecting on yourself is essential but should be undertaken with care. Most of the answers to critical questions in life are within us. So, keep enquiring yourself so that you can hold yourself on the right path. When you start questioning your inner self, acknowledge that you have taken your first step toward your growth.

The journey of a thousand miles will begin. We will start being more aware, more decisive, more confident, more happy and finally the ultimate fulfilment will be attained.

What are the most important areas of your life? Your career, health, family, and social life. Ask yourself which of these areas you would like to pick first. Yes, that is the first question. Prioritise the area that haunts you the most and the rest of the journey will be super easy.

CURRENTLY DOING

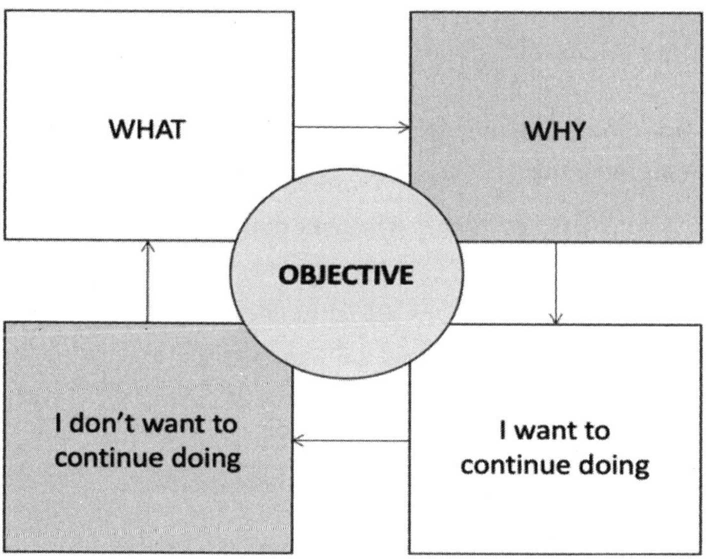

We will attain the current state of awareness. We will

ask many questions, and many will arise from the answers we choose. There is nothing right or wrong. It's your life and your perspective and yet I will advise you to put your question in a rhythm which will support sustainable building.

Look at these few questions. Read them out loud to yourself. Feel what you feel and say it to yourself or write them on a flipchart and see them until you start listening to answers from within. It's advisable to focus on any one given area of life at one time yet if they overlap don't be harsh. This is all yours.

❐ **The first aspect is, what am I doing?**

Why am I doing this?

What is my long-term objective in doing this?

Am I doing this only for the sake of doing it? Or do I really want to do this?

If I don't want to do this, why am I doing this?

❐ **Another important aspect to check into is what I am not doing.**

What am I not doing but want to do?

Why am I not doing this when I want to do this?

What cost am I paying by not doing what I want to do?

This journey of answering these questions from your inner core will require time and thought. Yes, the journey will not be a smooth one. There will be a time when you will see a mirage but you know what happens with a mirage. And what I can promise you will have multiple moments of Aaah! And for sure more Waah! You will realise many roadblocks and you will see many things in the blind spots. Once you do this you will come out with more awareness, more actions, and even more possibilities.

When you become aware of yourself, endless questions will pop into your mind. While engaging in an introspection exercise, you shall carefully listen to yourself, even the smallest thought should be explored, with no stone left unturned. Every pore on our body speaks to us. Every hair on our body speaks to us. Words are not the only way we interact with ourselves – it's a lot more than words. It's every pulse in our body that speaks with us.

1. What Am I Doing?

We all play different roles in our lives. Zara Habeeb is a gynaecologist. She is the doctor at her workplace and a caring mother, a loving wife, and a daughter-in-law at home.

She is well-praised by her patients. She takes good care of her home and family, and she has a very active social life.

When I met Zara, she was stressed as she was having the very same feeling. Am I missing something? Am I a good mother, a wife and a daughter?

Luckily, I got the chance to have a session with her about introspection, and I'm glad to say she ended up feeling really happy with what she's doing and she also discovered some areas where she can make improvements.

The first draft of the list of actions intentionally taken for the family looked like this:

1. I read a story to my children every night before bed.
2. I go out for dinner with my spouse fortnightly.
3. I spend at least one hour in the evening with my parents.

So, did you notice the word intentionally taken? Do you know what this means? We all do a thousand chores each day, and they require time and effort. But it is not enough for us. Then we take extra efforts and make some intentional actions. Again, there is nothing right or wrong – it was Zara's choice of what act she wanted to introspect first. Yes, there was a possibility that this list would keep on increasing from three to thirty or three hundred during introspection.

Make a list of all your actions but be mindful so that you are not overlapping your areas from family into a career or from business to social life.

Once you are ready, dive into the next question.

2. Why am I doing this?

To clarify your first question about what I am doing, it is imperative to ask yourself why I am doing this.

Once, I was waiting for my train at Delhi station. As

soon as the train reached the platform, all the passengers ran to board their respective coaches. The train was supposed to stop for ten minutes. That time was enough to board the train with your entire luggage. Still, people were running. They were pushing each other. Knowing that everyone had a comfortable way to board the train, why were they rushing? If asked this question, more than half the passengers would be clueless.

Something similar happens to us in everyday life. From the time we wake up in the morning to the time we go to sleep at night, we do several acts in every domain of our life. But, unfortunately, we are running to do all those things without asking ourselves why we are doing it or knowing how our act is impacting the lives of people around us.

Won't it be wonderful to know the motive behind our actions? So let us ask ourselves the following question in this exciting journey of knowing ourselves. Why am I doing this?

For example:

- I tell a story to my child every night to strengthen my relationship with him, and the act of mine gives me inner happiness.
- I go for dinner with my wife every fortnight to spend quality time with her and nurture your relationship and love.
- I spend at least one hour every evening with my parents to acknowledge their feelings, learn about their health and maintain a loving bond.

Remember, our aim is to complete this exercise in all four domains of your life — family, health, career, and social life. The fulfilment comes when we are happy in all four domains, and this can be achieved by the power of introspection.

Have you heard the statement, 'A mansion but no man' or 'I have billions but I am not happy.'

Most often we are after a wild goose chase because we don't know our purpose, our why. We can go for a long drive for a day in a week. But can we go for a long drive each day, with no destination decided, no purpose decided, not knowing the objective of the drive? Yes, I know people love long drives. But once a week is good. When we do it everyday it will lose the charm. Life is not to lose the charm. We need to live every day of our life happily, with something to accomplish, knowing what we are doing, and what is the objective of doing it. Isn't it?

As an introspective, let us ask ourselves the following question:

3. What is my long-term objective in doing this?

For example:

By reading storybooks to your child every night, you are trying to build a strong bond with them and receive immense pleasure. We all want to give a good upbringing to our children. We want them to achieve success in their life and, at the same time, stay connected with values. Moreover, you must spend time with your kids so they trust you and talk to you unfiltered.

The long-term objective is to stay connected with your family and become a friend and a guide to your kids, teach values so that you do not lose the relationship you share with them while they are growing up or moving ahead in their lives as adults.

Staying relevant in my relations is the long-term objective for me but the long-term objective differs from person to person. Everyone has their own version of wants and haves. Therefore, it cannot be taught but has to be discovered without judging yourself, and recording your reflections.

My purpose cannot be yours, and yours cannot be mine. But we all have a sense. With better perception, judgements will go, and you will start seeing your actions and work differently.

NOT DOING BUT WANT TO DO

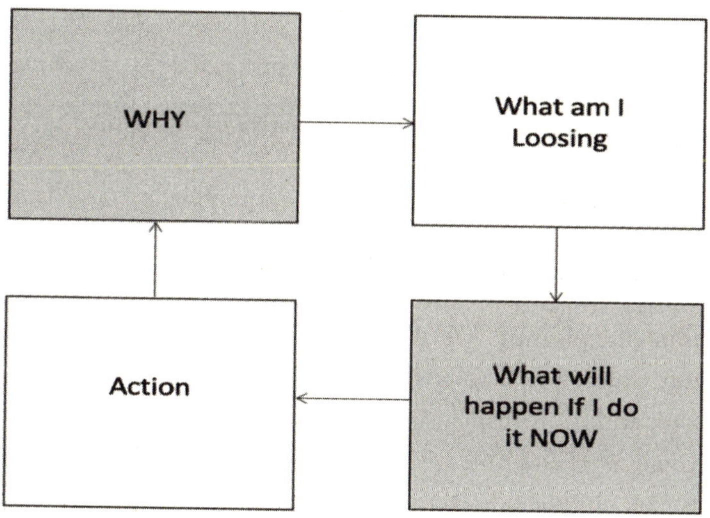

4. Am I doing this only for the sake of doing it? Or do I really want to do this?

Have you ever found yourself in a situation where you are doing the work only for the sake of doing it?

Priya was not used to getting up early. For a few years, she had Asthma. She was required to shed weight and lead a healthy lifestyle. Therefore, she started getting up early to jog for half an hour. Initially, Priya hated working out but was doing it for the sake of doing it. However, when she questioned herself, she knew she had a purpose in mind that kept her motivated. The active lifestyle improved her health, rejuvenated her, and boosted her confidence. Getting up early, meditating, taking morning walks, and doing yoga are now part of her morning routine. She now knows her long-term objective is to stay healthy and happy.

Add purpose to your efforts and see how your work efficiency increases. Increased work efficiency equates to improved work quality. Still, if the work quality is not falling on point, then you need to reason the purpose you have in mind.

No matter how much we try, we cannot give our best to the work we do not like. Often it becomes a very stressful situation due to irritability, and its effect starts falling into every domain of our life.

5. If you are doing something you do not want to do, before quitting, ask yourself;

Why have I been doing this?

Is it worth continuing to do this?

To put things into perspective, you need to know what you must and want to do. Priya was frustrated with her disease. She wanted to be cured but to do that, she had to adopt a healthy and active style. Knowing the purpose kept her motivated and she finally achieved her goal.

We often need clarification about where to focus in our lives – family, career, health, or social energy. To remove the confusion, check the other side of the coin. While doing this exercise of questioning yourself, you may realise that there are things that you are doing but do not want to do. In addition, there are a few things that you want to do but you do not do. Now it is time to look into them.

6. What Am I not doing but want to do?

Find some time and note down your feelings and thoughts. Analyse your current situation. Ask yourself what you are doing. Is this what you wanted to do in your life? Do you want to spend your whole life doing what you are doing now?

Sit down and close your eyes. Imagine yourself doing what you love doing the most. Then, write it down without any judgement or filter.

Explore this question, and you will gain clarity about things you want to do but are not doing.

It will help you get a fresh perspective and provide new ideas about what you want to do.

7. Why Am I not doing this when I want to do this?

Let's meet Ali, who is a dad to two lovely kids, Faizan, who is four years old, and Asma, who is two years old. Ali recently began a new business that keeps him very busy, and because of that, he can't spend as much time with his family as he would like. He feels sad and sorry about not being able to spend more time with his kids.

If Ali so much wanted to spend time with kids, why was he not doing it? He had the same excuse most of us have, 'I am busy, and I do not have enough time.'

However, you may have other excuses too, like

- Fear of rejection and failure
- Lack of motivation
- Procrastination, thinking that we will do it tomorrow, but tomorrow never comes
- Alternatively, because we prioritise other things over what we love or want to do

As in the case of Ali, starting a business and focusing on his career was his priority at present.

And here comes the need to ask the following question.

8. What cost are you paying by not spending quality time with your kids?

Will I be able to recover from this at a later stage? If not, what is the risk? Is the risk worth it?

In our fast-paced lives, we miss doing the essential things and unknowingly waste time indulging ourselves in activities irrelevant to our future. I know that so far, I have talked about only one domain i.e., family. In my experience as a motivational speaker and mentor, I have dealt with many successful business people or company executives who are now in their fifties. They have earned money and gained fame, but have lost the bond they used to share with their kids and spouses. They now live in fear of loneliness.

Indeed, career and social life are essential. The key is to be able to maintain balance. When we ask ourselves thoughtful questions, important realisations come into these domains.

Another significant concern is our health. We usually ignore our health when balancing careers, family, and social life. Yet, our body is a gift of God, and we must take care of it. A healthy body paves the way for a healthy mind. To attain every valuable resource, you need to be physically fit. Money can be earned back even if we lose it. But money can never buy back health once it deteriorates. Good health is an essential element of happiness. We must adopt habits that will lead to a disease-free life.

Anyway, we earn to provide necessities and luxuries to our bodies and stay happy. Then we get involved in the race to make more and more money. In this race, we often ignore our health, and our body becomes home to chronic diseases. Then, all the money earned is spent on your treatment. If your health is not good, you cannot enjoy the luxury money buys.

Many of us take a simple approach. We will care for our health once we have enough money. But we forget that we are ageing daily. Our metabolism is slowing down, and our bones are weakening. It is happening, and if we ignore our bodies from today itself, then after a point, our bodies will become so weak and unhealthy that there will be no energy left in us even to spend the money we have accumulated in the past.

Be responsible for your body. Think about where you want to be physically in a few years. Go through the process of questioning yourself in all four domains. Complete the exercise in all domains, and you will notice the blind spots. Be true to yourself to gain self-insight, and you will see more significant possibilities.

Chapter 2

Acknowledging Own Values

I very well remember that after completing the entire introspection exercises on the four life domains, I was restless. I was in the dark. I felt lost and had so many questions. I could not even sleep for some nights. The journey of knowing ourselves is not easy, but to bring about change in our lives, we need to stick to this journey.

Among the hundreds of questions that showed up, the one that perplexed me the most was: Why do I dislike a few of the things that I am doing?

Martha was the single mother of a lovely daughter, Nancy. To run her family, she worked as a bartender in a club. Her salary was good, and she got one day off every week. The club provides free dinner every day. The staff and her boss treated her very well. Every evening, the club was loaded with passionate men and women. Nevertheless, Martha did not like her job. On the other hand, for her sister and colleague Nicole, this workplace was no less than heaven.

How was there such a difference in the choices of both the close ones?

The answer to the above question is related to our values. Martha did not like to serve alcohol to people, while on the other hand, Nicole believed she was helping people to get a few moments of joy.

Martha's 'why' was deeply related to her values. Secondly, this job required Martha to stay at the club until 1 a.m., and Nancy would frequently miss her mother and her bedtime stories. Even though Martha desired to spend that time with Nancy, she needed to work to pay her bills.

I will avoid discussing which thought process is correct and whose thinking is wrong because, in that process, I may impose my values on you. Everyone has their own perspective and own values. Nothing is correct or incorrect until it harms society. What we need to understand is that our moral values determine our likes and dislikes.

Values are beliefs or principles reflected in a person's behaviour that help them to make decisions. Values are deeply held and shape a person's identity, purpose, and meaning. These beliefs that a person develops through personal experiences are acquired over time through education, cultural background, peer group influences, and family influences.

Values help you to differentiate between what is right and wrong for you in a culture, society, and community. Your values are the ideal standard of behaviour that allows you to set a goal in life.

Imagine standing in a queue at McDonald's waiting for your turn to buy yourself a burger. Suddenly someone cuts to the front. Everyone is taken aback. Few people complain but few stay calm. There are two different reactions to the same action. The person who cuts to the front may not value patience. But others who go by the queue value patience and fairness. Those who appreciated courage spoke up, and those who valued forgiveness decided to stay calm.

This is how different values shape our thoughts and actions. Talking about your values is an important step towards self-improvement. You may find many self-help books mentioning steps on how to achieve your goal but first, you need to know your values. If our goals are not aligned with our values they will not stay firm. Knowing our values can be compared with a compass that helps us find the direction we want to move. Our values guide us in career choices and other life domains and help us find fulfilment.

Examine your values whenever you feel stuck in your life while making decisions or choices. Be true to yourself, and you will know who you are. Knowing yourself will keep you adhering to the right path, will render meaning to life and determine your success.

Let me now take you to the day I attended a Co-Active coaching session with Ms Gonan about value alignment. I am sharing my experience because that session helped me understand the importance of values in life and assisted me in hunting for my beliefs.

At the start of the session, the facilitator asked, 'Do you know why you do not like a few things that you are doing?'

There was a long pause, as no one knew the answer.

The facilitator's second sentence was, 'because those few things do not align with your values.'

This was followed with the next question which was a bouncer.

'Can you write five values you live by?'

Believe me. Most of us were looking around to find the one courageous person who had raised their hand.

At that moment, my mind thought, 'Am I living a valueless life?'

I looked at the coach. It was as if our coach had read our minds by looking at our faces. She said, 'You are all in a dilemma in which you do not know what you know.'

To illustrate her above statement, she asked each of us to list situations in society that we could not tolerate. Then our minds unfastened, and answers started pouring out.

I remember myself writing few of the following situations:

- I cannot stand procrastination.
- I cannot stand lies.
- I cannot stand disrespect.
- I cannot stand rationalism.
- I cannot stand the negative attitude of people around me.

Moreover, the list went on, on, on, and on....

Complete your list of situations you cannot stand before you move to the next page.

I can't stand ______________________________

I can't stand ______________________________

I can't stand ______________________________

I can't stand ______________________________

I can't stand ______________________________

Life is all about learning something new. This learner's mindset keeps the door open for knowledge. I am always ready to learn something new. In this effort, I often listen to the lectures of other life coaches, mentors, and facilitators to brush up on my knowledge and experience.

During my Co-Active training days, when our coach Gonan asked us to write only five values of our life, we all were bewildered. But when she asked us to write acts or situations in society, that we could not stand, each one of us was ready with a long list.

This exercise has made it easier for us to acknowledge our values and weigh our ambitious goals to fulfil our values.

Gonan, then, asked us all to consider why we could not stand those situations, behaviours, or acts.

The point of acknowledging your values is to embrace them and not accept others' beliefs. Therefore, it is imperative to dig deep into yourself to discover why you cannot take certain societal behaviours, acts, or situations. The answer lies not in judging others but in understanding your values.

For example:

- You cannot stand disrespect because you value respect
- You cannot stand rationalism because you value humanity
- You cannot stand procrastination because you value commitment
- You cannot stand lies because you value the truth
- You cannot stand a negative attitude because you value positivity

How you behave in a particular state of affairs reflects your value.

Are you able to identify your values from situations you cannot stand?

Our understanding of good and bad reflects our beliefs. What we do in our career, relations, and personal lives rely on our values. Thus, it is crucial to mine our values.

The fundamental part of self-awareness is to know yourself and understand the world around you by having insight into your values. This will improve your communication skills, provide emotional regulation, and help you to become more empathetic. Nevertheless, defining your value is your top task. It requires self-honesty and deep self-reflection.

Let me make this easy for you by asking what you are doing and why you are doing it.

We do many things every moment. We may not realise it, but every time we take action, we direct our energy toward honouring some of our values.

For example:

- Every morning I listen to the audio book and introspect on how to use the lessons from it in my personal or professional life. Through this act of mine, I am valuing 'lifelong learning.'
- I always make sure that I arrive on time for all my meetings, and I honour my value of 'punctuality.'

We have already gone through the list of situations we cannot stand and we successfully mined a few of our values. It is time to discover our values from the actions we choose to take in our day-to-day lives and the patterns we follow.

Mining is all about diving into your experiences, patterns we follow and the way we behave. Take time and think about the experiences that have shaped you and what you have learned from them. Consider the challenges you faced and the values that helped you to overcome those challenges. Finally, consider the core beliefs that are most important to you. For example, it might include respect, kindness, honesty, or perseverance.

Think and consider how your priorities align with your core values.

On your journey of mining for your values, you need to observe your actions and identify a pattern that aligns with your principles and beliefs.

While sipping your coffee in the morning and evening, think about your recent actions and behaviours and consider what you did and why you did that. Be objective as much as possible, and be honest with yourself.

Do this exercise for a few days to discover recurring patterns in your behaviour that align with your values.

Natasha distributed free food to homeless people she met on her way to the office every morning. Even if she was not well and took leave from work, she made sure the food was distributed to needy people. She knew they would be waiting eagerly for her to bring them food. Think about it. Which value was she honouring here?

Nirdosh, another friend of mine, would never finish his tiffin in the office. Yet, he would neither take the food back home nor throw it away. If the tiffin was untouched, he would ask a colleague or the office boy to take it, or if it was leftover, he would feed it to a cow or a dog on the way from the office.

When I asked him why he went around looking for a cow and why he did not throw it away, he would say, 'I don't want to disrespect food.'

I asked him again, 'Why don't you take it back home and finish his next meal?'

'I do not want to disrespect the love of my mother, who cooks this every morning,' he replied.

Strange, but think about it. How many values is he honouring in this act?

Your task is to think about specific behaviours or actions you engage in. There can be several reasons behind an act of yours, such as personal preferences, social or cultural norms, or experiences that influence current beliefs, likes, and dislikes. Nevertheless, all of those actions reflect your values.

First, ask yourself if you are doing this because you feel pressure from others or if it is right for you. Next, define the motivation that drives your behaviour.

Along with understanding the motivation behind your actions, also analyse your emotions. For example, Natasha felt good after distributing food to the poor and needy. When your actions align with your values, you feel good.

All the above steps will help you to understand yourself and your values.

How would you want the world to look at you?

You will find the next part of the exercise quite interesting. Close your eyes take a deep breath, and imagine.

It is your sixtieth birthday, and your kids are organising a gratitude day for you.

In your life, you come across many people, and you will come across many more. You do certain things for them. After all, you live by your values. That is how you expect to be remembered.

Gonan asked us to keep our eyes closed and imagine what I expected people to tell me at my gratitude party. I had to take every name individually and tell what I imagined they had to tell me. What do they want to thank me for?

I saw:

- Reema, my batchmate from high school. She thanked me for always standing by her and helping her by sharing my notes.
- Gaurav, my cousin, and my best friend forever. He expressed gratitude towards me for his career guidance and mentoring him to achieve his goal.
- My college friend Shweta thanked me for standing up for her when her boss was mentally harassing her. She said thanks for standing by her side like a pillar, giving her courage, and getting the boss's true face revealed in front of HR.
- Moreover, I saw Robert, whom I encouraged to seek more from his life and motivated him to make

> efforts to acknowledge his skills. As a result, from being a peon he became a driver and then from a driver, he entered into sales. Today he is the sales manager at a Hyundai car showroom.

All the above glimpses from the past point toward my values and what I am doing or would like to do in my life.

Now, getting back to the Gonan's session. She was writing down all the values being reflected by our answers. After that, she gave me a red marker pen and asked me to reach out to the flip chart and highlight the four values that resonate most: Values that are behind what we do and want to do.

Soon there was a lunch break, but we were asked to stay in that mental space as the next part of the session would be to align our values with activities we have listed that we are doing in the four domains of our life.

Believe me, none of us could even relish half of the meal. Then, after lunch, we all returned to the room with heavy heads, fast-beating hearts, and butterflies in our stomachs. All the organs of my body, the brain, the heart, and the gut were synchronising.

To our surprise, our coach, in the next session, was changed to shift the room's energy. This may have been done to relieve us from the heaviness we all were experiencing.

Our next coach Nick asked us how our day was.

The only word we all in the room found appropriate to describe our experience so far was Deee…..ep.

Nick smiled and asked us to pull out the list of the things we were doing and quickly write the value which we felt we were honouring by doing that act, next to it.

We were again left to dive into the ocean of thoughts. The good thing was this time, we could find the value lined up with our acts.

Next, Nick asked, 'Is there any act for which you cannot identify the value you are honouring? If yes, think again, Why am I doing this? What is the cost I am paying for doing this?'

He added, 'While answering this question, remember that the time you spend doing the work is the first cost you pay.'

This was the time to write down a purpose statement for yourself. A statement, that will be a constant checkpoint for everything we do from now on.

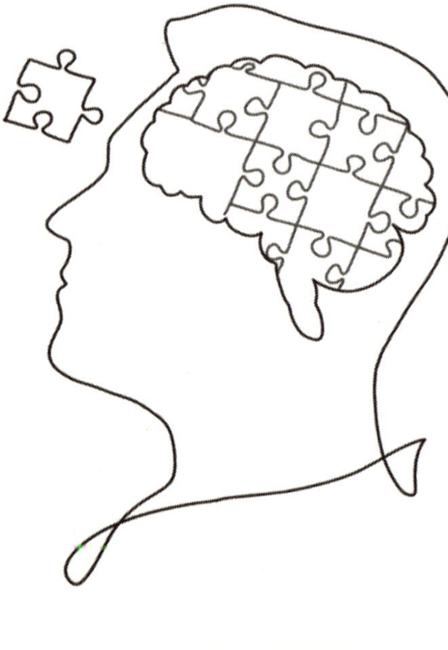

Start your purpose statement as follows:

I am .... Who is living to ....

While writing this statement, you have to follow specific rules. In the first blank goes a name (not of a human being, alive or dead) but something like a diamond, a river, a leader, a tree, a torch, etc.

You must wonder how to write a purpose statement considering yourself as a river or a torch. Seems interesting yet confusing. Isn't it?

I felt the same at Nick's session. So let me share the purpose statement I wrote that day and committed to evolving further.

> I am a river who lives to nurture lives around me. I never stop, even if I have to break into streams. Sometimes I can be very noisy. Other times, I am calm, but I will always continue to flow.

Today's evolved version of that statement is as follows:

I am the source to nurture others into living the life of a river, to nurture others into leaders, into good human beings. Nurture them to nurture others into such rivers.

It is time for you to write down your purpose statement that aligns your mission in life with your beliefs. This will help you clarify your goals and values and give direction to your life. In addition, a purpose statement will guide your behaviour and decision-making.

A purpose statement reflects your values after carefully

considering what is essential for you and what you want to stand for. In addition, it gives an idea about how your values are lined up with regard to your aspirations and personal goals.

A purpose statement is a powerful tool to achieve success as it clarifies motivation and direction. Aligned with values, it helps us to focus on our strengths.

Create your purpose statement that will guide your actions. You are more committed to your goals when you have a distinct sense of purpose. Likewise, it becomes easy for you to make resolutions that align with your drive. When your objectives are clear, you are more focused.

In addition, a purpose statement also helps you measure your progress from time to time and stay on track toward your goal.

I shared the entire experience I gained while attending the session with Gonan and Nick. Do the exercise on values. Write down your purpose statement, not just hang it on your clipboard or place it in your study table drawer and then forget about it. Instead, keep reviewing the purpose statement and assessing whether your actions are aligned. This way, you will stay committed and focused, and this is what you need to live a fulfilling life.

From this point on, anything you do will be for this purpose of your life.

I am ____

Who is living to ________________________________

____

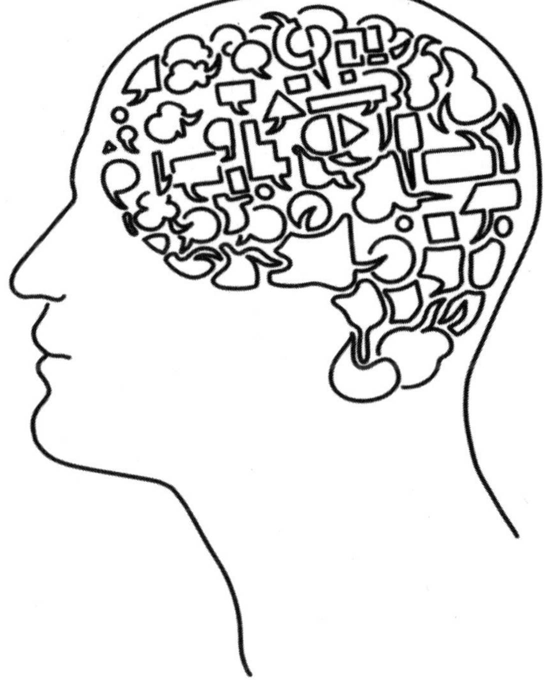

Chapter 3

Communication: How to Communicate

When I was in college, one of our professors asked the class a question.

'How many of you talk to yourself?'

Only a few in the class of sixty students, including me, raised their hands. Other students laughed at us. Finally, one could not resist and said, 'One who talks to self is crazy. You guys are crazy.'

Our humble professor, instead of snapping at the teen smiled, and to everyone's surprise, asked the boy to have a cup of tea with her after the class.

The boy paused for a second and then answered.

'Mam, I would have gladly accepted. But we have a test after this class.'

'Oh! my bad. But have you perceived that you communicated with yourself before answering me?'

If I am guessing right, you questioned yourself:

- Should I go out for a coffee with the professor?
- Moreover, what about the test?
- What will other students say? Will they laugh at me or call me a stud?
- Will the principal punish me later for skipping the test and having coffee with the professor?
- What if the complaint goes to the parents?

And finally arrived at the following decision:

- Ok, let me tell her no. But, I have to be gentle with

> rejection because I do not want to make her feel bad, or she will fail me in my assignments.

'Your communication with yourself was fast. It went on for a few seconds. Before you could realise this, you were ready with an answer for me,' the professor explained.

'We constantly communicate with ourselves,' she added. Everyone in the class was left dumbfounded.

Communication is a part of our existence, and both humans and animals communicate.

Have you ever questioned yourself about where this communication starts from?

Communication starts right in our heads. We are always chitchatting in our minds. Our mind works constantly. We are always bragging, planning, complaining, or thinking.

All this seemed normal and was not a concern until I was exposed to Neuro-Linguistic Programming (NLP), an experience that started a new chapter of my life.

Let me shed some light on its history for all of you who have never heard of NLP.

In 1970, two successful therapists and communicators, John Grinder and Richard Bandler, developed Neuro-Linguistic Programming to identify patterns in language and behaviour. They introduced specific techniques and communication approaches that allow you to connect with yourself and achieve desired outcomes.

The idea behind this is that our experiences shape our perception of the world. NLP techniques help us change how we think and communicate to bring changes in our behaviour. It helps to identify and overcome limiting beliefs, negative behaviour patterns, and other obstacles to success.

What was mind-blowing for me was the power of the subconscious mind, the power of understanding how our subconscious mind controls everything and how internal communication affects our present and future.

I will avoid getting deep into making you understand what NLP is. The information is available all over the internet. Instead, I aim to teach you how to use the NLP technique to reframe thoughts through various examples.

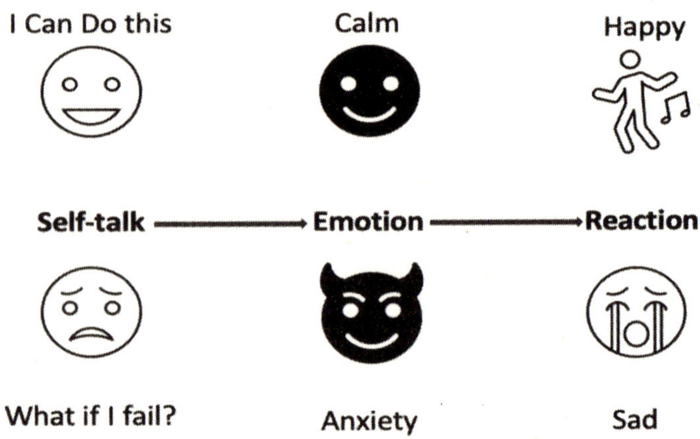

In this book, we will primarily focus on three sides of the communication.

- First is the internal communication

- Second is external communication
- Finally, the third side of communication is the result that our audience perceives from our message.

So let us start with internal communication.

Internal communication, or communication with self or self-talk, is an ongoing conversation in our minds. The constant voices we hear in our minds. These conversations are thoughts, feelings, and beliefs we express through our experiences, perceptions, and actions.

Self-communication serves as an essential tool in personal growth and development. When you reflect on your emotions, thoughts, and behaviour, you understand yourself better, which positively affects your life. Whenever you encounter a difficult or stressful emotion, talk to yourself. You will reflect on your experience and emotions, which helps you develop emotional intelligence and resilience. As a result, you cope with stress and bounce back to the challenging situation quickly.

Communicate with yourself about what you want to achieve and why. It will help in creating a road map for your personal growth.

However, it is vital to be aware of and pay attention to your inner dialogues as they significantly influence attitudes, behaviour, and emotions. For example, positive internal communication improves motivation, confidence, and resilience, whereas negative conversation with the self leads to self-doubt and criticism. Therefore improving your communication with yourself is the best way to improve self-confidence and create empowering and positive thoughts. In addition, it enhances creativity and increases your work efficiency and productivity.

Internal communication makes you more aware of your underlying beliefs and behaviour patterns. Moreover, it helps to identify the negative behaviour patterns and thought processes that might hold you back on the path to success. Once you recognise the recurring negative thoughts that keep your mind engaged, you can replace them with more empowering and positive ones.

Have you heard about the concept of the law of attraction?

What we think is what we become, and how we feel is what we get.

I'll make this clearer by describing a simple day when you oversleep.

Acknowledging you are late, your thoughts run, 'Oh my God! I am late today. Traffic would be heavier than usual already. I will undoubtedly miss the board meeting.'

If you start your day with this thought, how will it design the rest of your day? Let us have a look.

You start late for your office. You have self-talked and assumed the traffic would be heavier. So even if traffic is regular, you will be in that mindset that it's heavier and reach late for your board meeting. With unnecessary stress hovering, you forgot to bring essential files. As a result, you miss the meeting because your report is in that file.

Now, let us rewind this moment.

'Oh my God! I overslept. The board meeting will start at ten and I shall be late by fifteen minutes. What can I do? Let me call Rohit and ask him to fill in for me till I reach.'

You call your colleague Rohit, inform him that you are running late by fifteen minutes, and ask him to fill in for you until you arrive.

The result of this reference communication will leave you calm. You have sorted out the situation. In the end, you would have completed the fantastic presentation even if you were a little late.

We attract what we speak to ourselves. Therefore always be vigilant of your internal communication.

You've probably heard your grandparents and parents tell you not to say anything wrong as whatever we say may come true and something bad might happen. This advice from older people is connected to the way we talk to ourselves and something called the law of attraction.

The conversation going on inside you becomes the basis of your thinking. Your thoughts give birth to words and generate behaviour.

For example, suppose you are preparing for your exam. Although you have completed half your course, you repeatedly tell yourself, 'I am not preparing well and will forget everything I have learned.' This negative thinking creates anxiety and makes you waste the remaining time. Finally, you refuse to appear in the exams. Even if you sit for your exams, because of the incomplete course, you cannot complete the paper and get fewer marks.

Now reframe the self-talk. Convey to yourself that you have completed half the course well and that you are focused and will make the best use of the remaining time to complete the rest of the course. By saying this, you boost your confidence. You complete the course on time, confidently appear for the exams, and score well.

Alter how you communicate and purposefully utilise the law of attraction to change your life positively.

You generate misfortune by continuously discussing the circumstances and experiences that made you feel miserable. Instead, speak about the aspects of your life you are grateful for.

We all have a self-esteem cycle, and we are all controlled by the internal communication in our minds. Picture where you want to see yourself and choose your words wisely while talking to yourself.

In every life scenario, we face an 'Oh my God!' situation. Our internal communication might drive us to let us look into it. Life is uncertain. Unexpected things happen. Instead of expressing annoyance and frustration with a situation or a person, acknowledge the problem by saying, 'Let us look into it.'

Okay, let me make the statement simple for you.

If you are stuck in an unwanted situation, will you focus on the problem or the solution?

An unwanted situation can very quickly make you feel

overwhelmed. Avoiding the problem can make you panic, making things worse. This can be counterproductive.

Remember the lesser the time you take to shift from the anxiety state of 'Oh my God!' to 'Let's look into it', the easier life will be.

Thus, approach the situation reasonably and calmly. Choose more neutral and positive phrases. A solution-focused and proactive mind can lead to a more effective solution.

Approach the unwanted situation by being analytical and objective. Saying 'Let's look into it' helps us acknowledge the problem, enabling us to focus on areas that need attention. It signals that you are willing to understand and investigate the circumstances, creates a sense of control over the unwanted situation, and this approach helps you to make decisions to address the problem.

Consciously controlling your talk deliberately locks out negative thought patterns. Focus your internal communication on how capable or great you are rather than obsessing over your mistakes or constantly judging and interpreting your experiences. Remember, every experience in your life, whether good or bad, teaches you something and has helped you to stand as the person you are today.

Our biggest dilemma in the race for success is to compare ourselves with others. And by doing so, you waste the person that you are. Furthermore, constantly comparing yourself to others often makes you feel inadequate, leading to no self-worth and negative talks.

Monitor how often you use the words, I must, I should, or I have to in your everyday conversation with yourself.

Using these phrases creates a sense of pressure, guilt, and obligation. In addition, using these phrases makes you feel like you have no choice in the matter, which leads to stress and frustration.

For example, when you say to yourself, 'I will have to finish this project by today evening,' you might feel pressure to complete the project, leading to anxiety and stress. Try and rephrase it to 'I will finish this project today.' This is a decision statement and expresses possibilities.

Similarly, when you say, 'I should go for a morning walk tomorrow', you bind yourself to a task you should have enjoyed doing. As a result, if you fail to go to the park the following day, you feel guilty. Try and rephrase it to 'I love to go for a morning walk tomorrow. I will do some brisk walking.'

The power of positive paraphrasing is a way of expressing things in a more optimistic and constructive manner. Instead of using negative or critical words, we choose a positive and encouraging language. This helps in improving communication and building better relationships. For example, instead of saying, 'You're always late,' you could say, 'It would be great if you could arrive on time.' Positive paraphrasing can make conversations more pleasant and helpful for everyone involved.

Therefore, we should be very cautious while framing our thoughts. Monitor your opinion and rephrase your self-talk into empowering and positive language.

Instead of saying 'I have to,' say 'I choose to' and it will support you in pursuing your goal. Monitoring self-talk and selecting positive words gives you more control over your actions.

Remember, no one in this world is expected to be perfect. **Be compassionate with yourself. Eliminate the 'I should,' 'I must,' and 'I have to' phrases in your life.** I understand it may not be easy because you have these thoughts automatically, but the key to managing your thoughts lies in accepting your shortcomings and celebrating your strengths.

Think about some statements you would re-phrase in your daily life:

I have to________________________________

to____

I must do________________________________

to____

I should ________________________________

to____

Imagine how it sounds when we say to someone else, 'You have to', 'You must do', or 'You should do'.

How would your listeners interpret these words and phrases?

Therefore, when speaking to others as well as to yourself, avoid using these words.

The second part of communication is external communication.

How do you communicate with the people around you?

Communication is a fundamental part of human interaction. It plays a crucial role in our professional and personal lives, allowing us to share our needs, experiences and knowledge.

Recently I attended a program with Robin Sharma. He said, 'Keep conversations alive. Have conversations with your friends, family, and business associates, because communication is the key to keeping relations moist.'

But to communicate, you should learn how to converse and how to prepare.

Let me take you on a journey from 'what will I say' to 'what will they receive' to 'what will others perceive.'

Let us think of a situation.

A young girl badly wants to go on an international trip for ten days with friends. But her family is a little conservative and protective. Her chances of getting permission are slim. Gaining some confidence, she decides to put her desire before her parents.

What speech should she prepare to sound convincing to her parents?

How much preparation is required?

Here she needs to understand

What to say?

How to say?

When to say?

Have you watched the movie *'Dilwale Dulhania Le*

Jayenge (DDLJ)? If you are a 90s kid or have been an adult then, I am sure you would have watched. You never know how much you can learn from movies.

Remember the scene from the movie DDLJ where Kajol had to convince Amrish Puri and seek permission for the Euro trip?

She chose the perfect time when the family was spirited after the evening Prayer. Her desire was perfectly scripted with the blend of emotion, and her tonality was perfect.

The result was she got permission for the trip.

The question is do we always need an excellent emotional script for our communication?

How many times have you heard the phrase, think before you speak?

Well, this ubiquitous adage emphasises how important it is to consider the impact of our words before we say them. Thinking before speaking helps us to avoid saying something offensive or hurting while communicating.

Understanding others, and their perspective of the situation is even more important, as that will further help us prepare for our conversation.

The third part of communication is how our audience will perceive our message.

People see things differently, and they'll understand our message based on their own thoughts and feelings. The hardest part is figuring out how they see things.

Let me share with you a real-life situation.

Abdul belonged to a joint family and was settled in Mumbai. His family was in the business of manufacturing automotive spare parts. So far, everyone in the family had worked in the family business. Abdul just finished his software engineering and received an offer from California. He was emotionally attached to his family but also to his dream. He had to share this news with the family, and he was not sure how to tell them that he would be going far away from home. He was mainly worried about the feelings of his grandparents and parents.

I set up a room for this conversation with six chairs, four of which were currently empty.

I instructed Abdul to picture his parents and grandparents sitting in those four chairs, having just listened to his entire conversation. I made him sit in each of those chairs and express his thoughts and feelings from the perspectives of each of his four elders.

I kept noting the words he used relating to their concerns, fears, and beliefs. The majority of the keywords referred to were their concern for Abdul and some regret over his absence. Abdul shared his predicament with me after connecting through a mutual friend. He talked about what he was thinking, how important the job was to him, and his plans for the future.

The next step was to find out what his grandparents thought about this. I shared the keywords with Abdul and asked him to prepare his answers, which had a clear plan that addressed all those worries and addressed how he would still stay in touch with the family.

Just think about it, what if we could apply this approach to every conversation? If you remember the saying, 'Think before you act, as if this were happening to you,' you'll consistently find solutions.

One of my friend's mother had diabetes. We were at a party, and her mom wanted a glass of mango shake. My friend forbade her mother from having the shake saying, 'Control your taste buds, Mom, or you will die.' The daughter was worried, agitated, and frustrated but the choice of her words was too poor.

I know anyone would perceive my friend's statement as

rude. 'How can she talk to her mother like that?' However, my friend intended to ensure her mother's sugar level was within the limit. For the mother and the daughter, the conversation seemed regular. Nevertheless, my friend was at fault as her selection of words was not acceptable to spectators and this was not what she wanted to attract for her mother.

Just imagine if the mother was not in the mood to accept such a rude statement in public. How would she perceive your message? Could she get upset?

In any situation, it is advisable to do a three-dimensional perspective analysis of our communication. **The words we choose to express ourselves influence us, the person we communicate with, and the spectators who are present or observing the interaction.**

You might ask, 'How does it matter what the third person perceives from communication between two people?' The answer to this question is that communication is a social process within a larger social context. Therefore, the way two people communicate with each other affects how others perceive their relationship. In addition, persuasive communication may influence others to take a particular action or adopt a specific viewpoint. So, be mindful of how your communication with others affects those around you. Endeavour for inclusive and respectful communication.

Knowing your audiences' perceptions is one aspect, but understanding their learning patterns goes deeper. Neuro-Linguistic Programming (NLP), a science, has greatly aided my comprehension of my audiences' learning patterns.

While expressing ourselves or attempting to convey our message to others or in front of others, understand that there are three kinds of learners or perceivers.

- **Audio learners** – who tend to perceive and process the information better when it is presented in a spoken form through audio books, podcasts, and lectures. They usually benefit from discussion or repeating the information loud.
- **Visual learners** – who prefer information presented in a visual form, such as videos or diagrams. Creating mind maps also helps them to perceive knowledge in an organised manner.
- **Kinaesthetic learners** – Such people process information better and stay focused when interacting with it physically through role-play and specific activities.

Most people exhibit a mix of two, with one being dominant and the other a supportive trait. Thus, while communicating with others, it is preferred to know their communication preferences. This helps to tailor your communication approach to better suit the needs and preferences of your audience. This will result in engaging and effective communication. Moreover, that is what we want. To sound convincing while conveying information.

Remember communicating is not just about putting out your words all the time but also listening actively to your audience, listening to their questions, and responding thoughtfully to their concerns.

It would be best if you are prepared to anticipate and address objections. Consider all the potential objections your audience might raise and be ready with responses. In addition, use open body language by employing expressive gestures and eye contact. Through these tips, you can communicate effectively and improve your ability to persuade and influence people around you.

Chapter 4

Organising Time to Find Time

What is the most common excuse we encounter while working on any kind of growth plan?

Can you guess?

'I do not have time.'

Let us take a simple case of not returning your mother's call even after a week. It is bound to worry her, so she messages you, inquiring about your well-being and wondering why you are not calling or answering her phone.

Tell me your obvious reason for not being able to pick up her phone calls.

'Sorry, Mom. I was busy.'

Is this, however, true?

Yes! At times, we cannot attend a long call, but we can have a quick chat. But our belief, our comfort zone that we don't have time, makes it impossible for us to find that time.

Have you noticed how frequently we use the line 'I am busy' in our lives?

We talked about internal communication in Chapter three.

Consider how much time we waste when we constantly tell ourselves, 'I don't have time.'

- I cannot go for a walk because I am busy. Health is ignored.
- I cannot teach the kids because I am busy. Family is ignored.

- I cannot take on this project because I am busy. Business is ignored.
- I cannot go to this party because I am busy. Social life is ignored.

There are so many essential things to do that we probably do not realise that they are important and put a blinder on them by saying 'I am busy.' This is what brings dissatisfaction and causes unfulfilment in our lives.

I am sure none of us are doing this deliberately, and often this is the stage of 'I don't know that I know.'

I am certain that most of us have a busy schedule and multiple responsibilities. However, the belief that we are too busy can be a limiting belief that holds us back from making positive changes in our lives.

Would you like to explore the possibility of having time for everything you are doing along with everything you want to do?

Let us break this journey into three different parts:

1. Begin by saying, rather than 'I don't have time,' 'Let me work some time for this task on my calendar.'
2. Review what you have on your plate and make a list of all the tasks.
3. Delegate what can be delegated to others.

Challenging yourself to workout sometime on your calendar will help you identify new possibilities. It might involve learning new strategies, such as delegating the task to others or simply adjusting priorities to change your mind set and make time for what matters most.

You can set new goals by reviewing your schedule and using your time to align with your values and long-term objectives. This way, you can identify areas to improve your productivity and efficiency.

In order to overcome a challenge in areas like time management, communication, or self-reflection, you first need to realise that there's an issue. So, let me ask you, do you find time management challenging?

To take decisive action to win over any challenge, it is critical to first identify the challenge.

Often I am asked, 'How would I know that I am not managing my time well?'

Time is right there in between the task we do, and the jobs we can delegate. We just need an eye to identify.

I would reply by asking people to look at their daily routines and habits.

- Are you one of those people who is always in a rush?
- Are you the one who is never on time for meetings or social functions?

- Do you frequently need to catch up on deadlines?
- Do most of your family and friends complain about not being there?
- Are you forgetting where you kept those files or those car keys?

All these are glaring signs, often suggesting that the time has come to learn new techniques to manage your time better.

Lack of time management eventually leaves us burned out. Consequently, our health and careers are put in jeopardy, leading to diminished work, relationship issues, and lowered creativity. I am sure none of us would like to reach this stage or if already there, would like to move away from there.

So, what can be done?

The secret lies in time management. Time management is the magic mantra behind every successful business leader or entrepreneur. It assists in balancing multiple priorities by making the most of the available time. For example, Jeff Bezos, the founder of Amazon, has said that one of the most important things he does is to prioritise his tasks and focus on the most important things. He also delegates the job to others when appropriate. In addition, he emphasises minimising distractions and time-wasting activities.

You can follow a famous leader or a successful businessperson to learn time management skills, or you can look around yourself. You will find people efficiently dividing their time and managing every domain of their lives. Observe what they do differently. In my experience, I gained practical insight from my wife, Shalie.

My wife, Shalie Gupta, completes our family and is the real partner in my success. She plays a pivotal role in my work and the company I manage. On the one hand, when I often feel stressed out with too much work but not enough time in the day, she always seems to have enough time to do everything.

Once, I asked her, 'Why do I keep running out of time?'

'Because you keep everything in your mind and nothing in your notebook,' my wife replied.

I was looking at her as if she were speaking in some alien language. She said, 'Let me tell you what I do and how I reached this stage where I always find time to do everything I want, and you will understand.'

She reminded me of a few books and sessions we attended and how this has paved the way for her successful time management.

1. *The Checklist Manifesto* by Atul Gawande. This book talks about the importance of checklists in any project or business.
2. Delegation. We happened to hear a phrase in a Chinese movie, 'I don't do things that people can do for me. I do only things that I can do.' We kept laughing at these characters for days. On a different date, I was watching a video about the art of delegation with authority.

3. A session held by CJ (Chirantan Joshi), who shared with us the art of calendarisation.

This conversation was my first step in learning time management. I keenly looked into my wife's schedule and was dumbfounded at how effectively she managed every aspect of her life. Apart from being a mother, wife, and home manager, she is the general manager of a company. Despite her busy schedule, she even managed to find time to help me grow my business. With so many things on her to-do list, she still knows where she has time to attend spiritual gatherings and social parties.

Let us go through the journey of organising and finding all the time you need.

Checklist:

- To get rid of the fear to forget, checklist is my friend.
- To get time for everything I want to do calendarizing is the mantra.

The first step is to make a checklist for three months. You can play with two things together. First, create a three-month checklist that includes everything you are doing **repeatedly** daily, weekly, monthly, and quarterly.

Include everyday morning duties, sleep routine, social commitment reminders, activities planned with the kids, phone calls to our parents and relatives, changing the Wi-Fi password, and changing the bank password etc.

Yes, we are going to have a vigorous checklist of minor things. Eventually, this will lead to developing the habit of putting everything on the checklist. This very step will make the life stress-free. You will no longer be worried about forgetting something because whatever needs to be done is on the list and eventually on the calendar.

The idea is simple. List everything practically for the first three months. Having a statement about our schedule will help us prepare our to-do list and prioritise things for our day-to-day life.

Furthermore, keep previewing and revising your checklist to stay focused on your priorities and make necessary amendments.

Once the checklist is prepared, highlight the items or tasks you can delegate to someone else. Remember, if you keep doing things others can do for you, when will you do something only you can do?

Think about it.

Delegation

Delegation allows you to assign tasks to the people who have the necessary knowledge or skill to complete them. This will free your time to focus on things that are more important. If you continue to handle tasks that others can do on your behalf, when will you find the time to focus on the things that only you can do?

Nevertheless, delegation comes with a little risk. So we must gradually delegate with calculated risk. Thus, the first step is identifying the task that can be delegated, i.e., the time-consuming task that only occasionally requires your expertise or skills.

The biggest mistake is to delegate without authority, which might lead to conflict and confusion. Doing so, you might even undermine the accountability of those responsible for the task. Instead, speak to the appropriate person or team to seek inclusion and discuss with them why you believe specific tasks should be delegated to them, providing reasoning for your suggestions.

Once you have delegated a task, trust the person to complete it. Micromanaging can be counterproductive. For example, imagine you have assigned a task to your executive assistant or any other staff member to prepare a quotation. When the quote comes back to your desk for review, you may find a minor grammatical mistake that does not make any difference to the entire purpose of the letter. Still, you make the changes and sent it back for correction.

At this point, ask yourself, 'Was there a blooper? Would that letter have killed the deal? If not, was it necessary to change those words or correct that punctuation mistake?'

We do not even realise it, but this act, resulting from a lack of trust, shatters the team's confidence and blocks their way to fulfilling the purpose. Therefore, delegate tasks with authority and trust. Focus on systematic delegation, i.e., first give the team a small charge, then a bigger one, and then another more significant job. This way, we train our team to have the confidence to deliver.

Here are some tips on how to delegate effectively:

- Identify the task – Choose a person who has the skills to do the task and knowledge about it.
- Set alliances, communicate effectively and clearly and explain your expectations and deadline. Make sure the person understands and agrees with what is required.
- Provide support and guidance when required. While doing this, avoid taking over the task altogether.
- Finally, evaluate the result. Then, provide **constructive feedback** to help the person improve knowledge and skills for future tasks.

Be conscious of the economics of delegation. That is the time you will spend doing all those tasks which can be assigned to someone else is more expensive than the money you will spend on this person.

I will share my own experience with this. I used to drive around the town for my meetings and had no time to reply to my emails, strategise, or even connect with my family. One day my wife Shalie questioned me, 'Pankaj, how many hours do you spend driving and finding a parking spot?' I replied, 'Nearly two hours each day.'

'This means you spend at least fifty hours per month driving and parking, which equates to nearly one week of working hours.' She looked into my eyes and asked me another question, 'How much will it cost if we hire a driver?

Don't you feel you can utilise your time better while he is driving for you?'

Seriously, I never thought of it this way. Now it is nearly ten years since we hired a driver, I am utilising my travel time to give WhatsApp replies, answer emails, review consignments, and call my family and friends.

One more thing. If it is challenging to find the right person for delegation, it is better to spend a hundred hours finding and training the person than to spend six hundred hours in a year doing what they can do for you. After all, time is all we have.

Through the process of delegation, ideally, thirty to fifty per cent of your checklist can be assigned. And that is good news, so what to do with the rest of this checklist?

Let us put them on our calendar.

Calendarisation

Effective **calendarisation** is an art.

First, we need to categorise the remaining tasks into the priority framework.

High Priority: Priorities in our lives directly relate to our values. It differs from person to person. In this category, I personally keep the actions that are hundred per cent aligned with my purpose statement.

Urgent: Work that was not on our checklist but appeared unexpectedly falls into this category. We are all aware that unforeseen occurrences happen and that uninvited tasks that require immediate attention may appear on our desks. Determine whether those urgent tasks can be delegated before tackling them. If delegation is possible, delegate.

If not, you must determine whether or not the task is important enough to be prioritised over the task on schedule. If not, they will be incorporated into another to-do list, which is **'When a client cancels the meeting.'**

Still, make sure to have some blank time on your calendar each day. For example, after every meeting, block about 20 minutes. This is the free time for those chores that would come to your table unannounced.

Others: This includes client relations time, personal stuff you want to accomplish, and many more based on our various profiles and work lives.

The categorisation of tasks is very helpful in business. When we divide our office hours according to prioritisation, time management becomes much easier. When we divide our working hours into these blocks, we give thought to the importance of tasks that put the management of our time in our hands.

Once this process is complete, you need to enter each of these tasks on your calendar, giving them the time required. For example, I will block not only the meeting time but also the travel time to the meeting.

Once you fill in your calendar, you will notice the times that are free, and more importantly, you will soon be able to understand the actual time required and blocked may vary. Your skills will evolve over time. Remember, we have 168 hours of work per week, and when tasks are aligned with our purpose and our vision, we will steal time from ourselves.

How many of us are guilty of not meeting our kids because we come late from work, and the kids are asleep? Or when they go to school, and we are asleep? Kids are kids. They need to sleep early, but if family is our value, we can steal an hour from our sleep. It is just a habit. I stole nearly three hours and thirty minutes from my sleep to dedicate it to my passion, by waking up at 4.15 a.m. instead of 7.45 a.m. Did that happen in one go? No, I started stealing thirty minutes at a time. Great things start with small steps. Take the first step today.

Chapter 5

THE PERSONAL GROWTH PLAN

I recall spending summer vacations with my family in the holy city of Haridwar. Even today, for me, the ambience of evening prayer at Haridwar remains an everlasting memory. Prayers were being chanted loudly, bells were ringing, and the Ganges' waves were illuminated by twinkling lamps.

A couple of years back I had a chance to revisit the experience with my cousins. After the evening prayer, my cousins and I were sitting on the stairs of those temples and our feet were soaked in the flowing water of Ganges. Few of those enchanting lamps were still floating on the waves. All of a sudden my cousin Sanjeev asked, 'So, Pankaj babu what is your personal growth plan for this year?' For a split second, I was surprised because Sanjeev had never asked such a question before. Sanjeev, as if reading my mind, said, 'Don't be surprised. I attended a seminar last month, and I know you're always interested in such topics, which is why I asked you this.'

I felt awkward because Sanjeev was nearly twelve years my senior, but then I took control of all my emotions. I replied, 'Bro, I have created a vision for my BNI business and would like to impact two thousand lives by the year 2025. For this year, I plan to launch two chapters and grow my existing chapter by another 100 members. I am also planning to move to a villa from my apartment and buy another car. Maybe a Tesla. On the other front, I am working on exploring the possibility of starting a new business of 'Executive Coaching.'

'Wow, that sounds great,' Sanjeev responded, 'But my question remains unanswered.'

I apologised, 'Sorry, I couldn't understand. I told you everything about my growth strategy.'

Sanjeev stated, 'Bro you told me your business growth plan, your living standard growth plan, you're automobile growth plan. But my question was about your personal growth.'

'Do you agree everything around us is connected with us and grows because of how we think, how we behave, and how we manage?' he questioned.

'Of course,' I replied.

'Do you also agree that success depends on how much we grow in our learning and experience to overcome new challenges?' Sanjeev continued. 'This is why my question to you is not about professional or financial aspects of your growth, but I am asking about:

Physical growth

Spiritual growth

Mental growth

And

Emotional growth.

Personal growth has many domains and different faces. In our growing years, being promoted to the next class, gaining an inch of height, or learning a new skill are all growth for us. Once we cross the stage of our general academic year, having a job, starting a business, or joining a family business is growth. After that, getting married and having kids is growth for us.

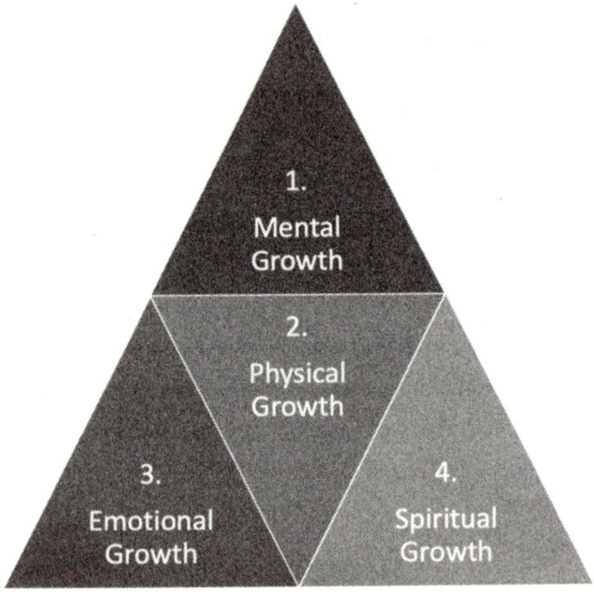

Every year, we make new plans. Some of them are executed, and we retain a few. Then, the following year, we set new goals and work towards them. Therefore, the process of growth is ongoing. The journey of personal growth never ends because there is always room for improvement in all aspects of life. It is a continuous process of developing new skills, improving unique qualities, engaging in self-reflection, and becoming more self-aware.

There is always new information to take in and a new challenge to overcome.

Success, happiness, and fulfilment come only when we invest our time in personal growth and development. When I say personal, it includes you and only you—not your career, balance sheet, or family—but your growth plan. Think of it as a spiritual, physical, emotional, and mental transformation that will positively influence you and enhance your overall well-being.

Self-growth is about being aware of your identity and addressing your attitude, values, behaviour, wisdom, actions, and habits to live your life to its tremendous potential. Your growth should always come first because it means you can show the world an extraordinary version of yourself.

Personal growth is a tool you need to survive in this ever-changing world. Becoming a better version of yourself is the key to attaining peace, becoming productive, and achieving success in every domain of experience. The possibility of self-growth is infinite, as you can grow whichever way you choose.

When focusing on self-improvement, there are many tempting options, making it challenging to pick one. The process first starts with self-awareness and culminates in targeted changes to oneself. With the right mindset, tools, and support, we can overcome any obstacle hindering our self-growth and ensure a positive outcome.

The self-growth journey will take effort. To unlock your limitless potential, you must come out of your comfort zone and make a significant life shift. This will require both patience and discipline.

After all, gold becomes pure only after penance in fire.

My question still stands unanswered. What is your personal growth plan?"

I was amazed by the line of thoughts and completely agreed with Sanjeev, and at this time if there was anything which could fit into this category was my recent enrolment to become a Maxwell Leadership Certified Team member. I shared my plan with Sanjeev and asked him more about this seminar which he had attended. He was very happy to share his journey, and we continued.

Have you ever felt like you were living a monotonous life and calling for a change? This stuck feeling where you find yourself not progressing and lacking direction, confidence, and motivation? This is a clear indicator that you need a growth plan.

Feeling stuck in life can manifest in many ways. For example, you might feel like you are not tapping into your creative potential. You might have a passion for art, writing, or other creative endeavours. But you are not making progress, as you do not know where to start.

You are not alone in experiencing being stuck. We all do that at some point in life. The good thing is that it helps to embark on your development in four domains of your life i.e., physical, emotional, mental, and spiritual. The want to improve your skill, knowledge, attitude, etc. creates the roadmap to help you achieve growth.

Personal development comes from the inside and is unique for every person. What important is to focus on what you enjoy about your life. It is about pursuing clarity and passion in life to achieve the purpose. Thus, examining your reason for the want of attaining the highest level of self-awareness will keep you motivated throughout. However, before you start on a personal growth plan, it is important to acknowledge what it entails. To reach self-actualisation means improving in all areas of life: mental, physical, spiritual and social.

What do you say, now? Would this be correct to say that all these areas are interlinked? We often have the scope to grow in every field. When it comes to personal growth – the sky is the limit. The most beautiful part is, there is a ripple effect. When you bring improvement in one area of your life, you will find that every other area of life has also improved.

To understand this a little better, let's see how Priya's small step unleashed the possibilities for her growth. Lack of driving skills made Priya depend on her husband or apps like Uber and Ola. She very much wanted to join yoga classes or learn music. However, even for small errands, she was dependent on others. Yes, her husband Vikas would often drop her off at her destination, but not always, and somehow she was never comfortable booking a taxi. Priya wanted to do many things in life, but this dependency was forcing her to bury her desires. She was stuck, lacked confidence, and was not happy with herself. Priya, too, was a participant in the personal growth seminar that I was attending. She was there for the second time. She shared with us that attending the seminar about the personal growth plan had awakened her from deep inside, and as a result, she chose to let go of her fear of driving and upgrade her skills. Coming out of her comfort zone and learning to drive was difficult, especially because she had a phobia of crossing roads that resulted from an accident during childhood. However, her strong desire to do something for herself kept her motivated. She learned to drive within one month. After practising for a few more months, she mastered driving the car. The freedom from dependency enabled Priya to dig out her buried desires. She was able to do things that were always on her list. She joined the music and yoga classes. Her confidence boosted her personality. With regular yoga practice, both her body and mind became healthy. Moreover, music connected her body and mind with her soul contributing to spiritual upliftment. The action she took for her personal growth in one domain changed every aspect of her life.

This realisation astounded me, and nearly three years later, I am sharing my experience with you. The biggest difference it made for me was that I realised the goal of self-actualisation is to get a little bit better each day. I began working on various aspects of my life, beginning with my physical health. I was nearly ninety-seven kilos when I started, and I am now sixty-five kilos. I maintain a gym, meditation, Pilates, golf, and book-reading routine. I've been concentrating on improving my abilities. And, yes, I wanted to learn to play the guitar but later realised it wasn't for me. My guitar, however, remains on a wall as a reminder.

So let us cover all the domains of the growth plan. You have probably heard people say that the mind, body, and soul are all interconnected. Our physical health affects our mental and emotional well-being, and vice versa. What do you think? Should we start the journey of self-development by improving our physical health? What is that physical development plan you have been burying under years of detritus? If not, what do you hope to accomplish in the next twelve months?

The first step is to be willing to work on improving yourself, and the second is to assess your current performance. Then, make small goals to achieve bigger physical changes that will subsequently affect your development on a mental, spiritual, and emotional level.

Maintaining physical fitness by eating right and working out, is not only physically healthy but also contributes to overall personal growth. Being physically active not only keeps your bones and muscles strong, controls your body weight, and improves your brain function, but also improves your mood, boosts your energy, helps you have better sleep, and improves your sexual life. When you are healthy, you feel confident, which is the most underrated benefit of having a good body. The best part is that the physical body is an excellent place to learn and develop the principles of growth planning, as you can see it and measure the progress.

In addition, when you work on your physical fitness, you develop self-discipline. Give a thought to the person who pushes you to quit smoking. Probably your spouse, your children, or your doctor. There are only a few who care, but even they cannot actually do anything unless you choose the personal growth journey for yourself.

Right away as you make a choice, exercising the necessary self-regulation no longer presents a challenge for you. Instead, because you are driven, it comes naturally. Any journey towards making that long-awaited physical change is not only your step towards physical fitness but also helps you master self-discipline and adopt other better habits that help you grow in other areas as well.

Let us have a look at the other areas of the personal growth plan:

Mental Growth: The basis for a healthy body and healthy emotions is a healthy mind. A mind free from worry and trepidation is directed toward goals. Mental health is an important aspect of overall health. Poor mental health can have a negative impact on every facet of our lives, including relationships, work, and personal fulfilment. Cultivate a more positive mindset, which will help us stay motivated and focused on personal development. Good mental health can help you develop the resilience you need to deal with whatever life throws at you.

There is a book called Authentic Happiness by Martin Seligman, in which he writes about positive psychology and 'The power of positive emotions.' One must read this book to work on our mental growth. In the book, the author explains that when we are physically healthy, we will have a healthy mind, and this can empower us to cultivate positive emotions.

This book helped me find positives in my failures. It helped me be at peace because I learned something new. I would not say I would never slip into emotions. Yes, I would feel bad. But what was important was how quickly I could come out of it with my golden nugget of new learning. Isn't that a healthy mind?

Spiritual Growth: Self-actualisation is a holistic process where you need to connect to yourself and find inner peace. Therefore, spiritual growth matters. It does not matter what approach you choose to grow yourself spiritually. All the techniques have the same effect of providing you with self-awareness and giving you a break from overthinking and from the continuous thoughts and sounds in your head that distract you. As a result, you can sleep well, improve your focus, and become more productive.

I had the opportunity to attend Vipassana in Ras Al Khaimah, UAE. Initially, I thought they would have some kind of chanting, meditation, and prayer. However, I was surprised by what I heard about it. I got a request to pick up Saad, who practised Islam as a religion and had come from Saudi Arabia to attend Vipassana. During my long journey with Saad, she shared that this was her second time practising Vipassana. Somehow I got comfortable and asked my stupid question, 'Is this allowed as per Islam to attend something like Vipassana?' She smiled and asked me if I had done any research about Vipassana.

I said no. It was just that my friend Mohit attended it, and I got excited about the idea of ten days of silence and staying away from my mobile. She then stated that Vipassana is a universal technique—a way of knowing oneself—that is non-sectarian, without any unquestioned faith or connection with organised religion.

The experience of Vipassana helped me connect with my body and bring awareness to my breath. Something that has been there with me since my birth yet is far away from my conscious self. It was a different level of spiritual connection that I developed with myself.

Practicing spirituality creates a sense of acceptance. It brings us closer to our real selves and connects us to our inner core. My friend Karan draws this from playing golf and through that reconnects with himself. He is completely focused, thinking only about direction and distance, visualising the shot he will take, and believing in himself to achieve what he has envisioned. Isn't that an unusual manifestation of spirituality?

Spirituality is an expansion of our consciousness to enrich self-awareness. It can be a different journey and different experience for different people.

Emotional Growth: When it comes to achieving all-round happiness in life, emotional intelligence is as important as intellectual ability. Learning to manage your emotions and respond positively to stress, assessing impact swiftly, and communicating clearly helps to overcome adversities. The ability to manage your emotions begins with self-awareness. The more you become aware of your emotions, the better you understand how they affect your behaviour and thoughts, and this helps you to understand your inner strengths and weaknesses, which can be fairly empowering.

Recognising each area of personal development is crucial to creating a growth plan because it allows you to assess where you are right now and the type of person you want to be. To realise your potential, this will help you identify your strengths and areas for development.

Now that we have discussed each area of life that should be included in our growth plan, let us learn how to create a simple personal growth plan.

To begin with, develop a clear vision of the kind of person you want yourself to become in the next twelve to twenty-four months. You may not be certain, but writing may help you gain clarity.

Analyse yourself. Write down your purpose, your beliefs, what inspires you, your **personal** areas of strength and areas that require improvement. Develop a vision that will help you make conscious decisions that align with your values so that everyday you are empowered to make little changes that assist you in achieving your goals.

Examine where you stand currently with your vision. Reflect on yourself. Self-reflection and self-awareness will help you identify the areas you need to improve and the skills you need to learn. Make your vision realistic by conducting a reality check that allows you to build an attainable plan to reach your goals. Keep track of and monitor your progress to stay focused. To keep distractions at bay, prepare a to-do or not-to-do list.

Including a new task or activity in your routine initially may seem tough. Start slowly, one thing at a time, and let the activity or task become your new habit. Yes, keep measuring the progress of your growth plan to stay responsible.

At times, it is advisable to have someone with you, who understands you and with whom you can share your thoughts and toss your ideas at them. Do remember that personal development cannot be achieved overnight. It is an evolving process that includes several steps.

Sustainable growth comes when we groom ourselves internally. The journey of my self-actualisation started by acknowledging my values and by making my life purpose statement. However, I had two options like everyone else:

- First to get my life purpose statement printed and framed and hung on the wall.
- Second, take conscious steps to grow and make an effort towards fulfilment.

I wanted to relax my mind from continuous overthinking and flashing good and bad memories. I wanted to calm my mind from the continuous talks and sounds running through it twenty-four hours a day while conversing with others, at meetings, and even during sleep.

On the spiritual side, I always wanted a guru to guide me in my journey of knowing my needs and help me to consciously correct my inner self.

I wanted to improve my relationships with my family members and friends, who were left behind during my journey of external growth but were always present in my subconscious mind. This made me emotionally drained.I wanted to be physically fit to have the energy and strength to do whatever I wanted, such as climbing mountains, scuba diving, or bungee jumping, and most importantly, I wanted to get rid of those painful muscle cramps, and fear of becoming diabetic.

I wanted to learn new skills, improve my leadership qualities, write a book, and learn to say sorry. I wanted to acknowledge how I impact the lives of people around me and how I behave. I want to learn to show gratitude and love.

In all these years, while I focused on my external growth, I left behind my inner self. But once my life purpose statement and my values were clear to me, I started growing personally in spiritual being, physical health, emotional health, and mental health.

When drafting your growth strategy, take into account every facet of your life. You cannot drive a car which has only three wheels. If you are empty inside, you cannot be fulfilled. Pause your busy life for a moment and take a look around.

- People with abundant wealth but no health
- Millionaires living alone in their mansions
- People standing in a crowd and yet alone with no one to share their hearts with
- People ill-treating others, leaving behind suffering, hate, or jealousy

Think about it and reflect upon your life. Discover the needs of your life and how you would like to work to become the best version of yourself. Develop healthy behaviours, and live a more fulfilling life.

Chapter 6

DECLUTTER

Congratulations! You have come halfway through the journey of unleashing success. On the path to unleashing our inner potential, we have examined our values, developed a purpose statement, and improved our communication skills. We have changed our belief system about time. We now know there is time for everything that we want to do, and while developing our growth strategy, we gathered memories and experiences.

The next step is decluttering, and this is not something new. It has been there for generations.

When I was a child, around a month before Diwali, I recall how my father used to inform my mother that Karamchand, the painter, was going to visit on such and such a date. This discussion between my parents was a reminder to make plans and take initiative. For both the inside and exterior walls of our home, we used to choose different colours. Each repair was detailed. The carpenter, electrician, and plumber were lined up. Additionally, every room in our home was emptied one by one before Karamchand's scheduled visit. The trunks, wardrobes, beds, mattresses, and drapes were all removed from the room.

While Karamchand painted the space and applied whitewash, we were given the duty of choosing:

- Which of the items needs to be preserved in its current state?
- What has to be fixed?
- What is damaged beyond repair and should be sold to a scrap dealer?

- What clothes we no longer wear and, can be donated or traded with the hawkers for steel utensils and pans?

All the extraneous items were either thrown away or traded for something helpful. Our closets were rearranged. Furniture was polished, painted, or mended. The home would be meticulously cleaned. Spider webs with dead insects and cockroach eggs were cleaned, and the mouse nests were all cleared from every nook and cranny of the house.

It took roughly three to four days to complete the cleaning, repairs, junk removal, and whitewashing of the house. Our home used to be prepared for Diwali and would look brand new.

I am sure remembering my childhood has drawn you all back into yours. As Diwali drew near, we all began to clean our homes, and this custom is still followed today.

That is why, as a child, I associated Diwali with house cleaning. However, when at school I was taught that the reason we celebrate Diwali is because Shri Ram returned to Ayodhya on this day after defeating Ravana, contrary to what I had previously believed, I couldn't relate. I couldn't find any link between the Diwali celebration and the annual decluttering process. It turned into a concern for me. I expressed my concern to my father when I got home from school. My father responded to this inquiry of mine in a way that I can still clearly recall. 'My dear son,' he replied, 'Diwali symbolises the spiritual triumph of good over evil and of knowledge over ignorance. Diwali is a festival of sharing joy and spreading goodwill.'

Diwali celebrates the emergence of a fresh start. However, how can we begin a new chapter in our lives if we do not get rid of the outdated clutter in our lives or mend it? How can we go forward?

Diwali is an annual occasion for us to declutter our homes. If we don't get rid of the old, broken items from the house each year, clean the cobwebs, get rid of the mouse nests and cockroach eggs, and have the walls painted, then eventually, we'll be living with a mountain of trash, a horde of pests, and the same boring wall colour all around. By decluttering the house once a year, we can get rid of unnecessary objects, fix broken goods, and replace what we no longer need with what we do. This is how we plan to be joyful, focused, and cheery in the coming year.

I was able to fully comprehend everything my father said. At least, that is how I felt then. I understood everything my father told me about the link between Diwali and cleanliness.

With time in life, we tend to collect more and more baggage on our backs that is no longer useful. Decluttering is a process of letting go.

Decluttering simply means letting go and moving on from the negativities that have hurt you, letting go of the experiences that do not exist in the present and the memories that chain you.

Imagine your mind as a room filled with boxes named finance, relationship, career, bill, taxes, health, past, present, future, failure, desire, and so on and on. You see, the room is filled too much. There are too many boxes, and not much space is left for new boxes.

Can you imagine a library where books are not stacked and indexed? Can you really find the book you are looking for before hustling with many other books? The same goes for our minds. When we clutter our minds with too much information, memories, expectations, desires, etc. Our brains hustle with all of them before finding what is actually required. Even your computer or phone hangs or does not work when too much is stored.

Take into account how a decluttered brain can help us achieve our growth objectives. In 2003, I was going through a rough patch in my life, and the business was going through its downfall. I was drowning in worry and lost in my thoughts.

My father noticed my anxiety and one day sat next to me during evening tea and asked, 'What's the matter? What is the cause of your current anxiety?'

I told him about how my business was slowing, how my deals had gone off track, and how I lost money in business.

'I was doing so well in the USA. Why the hell did the 9/11 attack happen? Why did I choose to come back to India?'

My father stared at me and asked, 'Do you remember what we used to do every year before Diwali?'

I responded, 'Yes, we used to declutter and reorganise the house and paint the walls. Why are you asking this question? Isn't Diwali still a few months away?' I was curious.

My father responded, 'It's not about this house. It's about you, my son.'

'When was the last time you decluttered? I am not referring to your room or wardrobe. I am referring to your inner self. You must clear your mind of negative thoughts and memories to make room for new skills and positive thinking as you prepare for new challenges.'

My father drove me to process my first decluttering when I was twenty-three, and that was one of the best lessons I received from him.

Let us come to a halt, concentrate on our thoughts, and try to silence them.

Pause

Pause

Pause

Pause

Question: When was the last time you decluttered yourself?

Recently, while learning for my certificate in Co-Active coaching, I came across a programme called 'Process,' and the magic key is, 'How Is This Helping Me Now?' It makes it simple to find our inner calm and purge our inner clutter.

Are you prepared to purge the clutter from your life?

Examine the four rooms of your inner home, which include family, health, and social life. Now, choose any room where you want 'Karamchand' to work.

Take a pile of the slips and make small notes, one slip for each thought, memory, belief, and sound from your mind, and do this until the room is empty for whitewash. In this space, pick any colour you like. While Karamchand is whitewashing and painting, we will repair, polish, discard, or exchange an item for another useful one.

If you have any albums, gifts, or souvenirs from your past, put them on your table. Each of these items holds memories and beliefs, and today, we want to take a look at them. One by one, pick up each note you have made and ask yourself, 'How is this assisting me right now?' By asking yourself, 'How is this helping me now?' you can finish cleaning the first room of your inner self.

When we ask ourselves this question, it allows us to pause and reflect on the present moment. We can look at the thoughts or memories that are occupying our minds and ask ourselves whether they are useful in our current lives or causing unnecessary stress or anxiety. This allows us to start identifying and letting go of thoughts or memories that are no longer useful or relevant. This will help to declutter our minds and improve our ability to focus on the present moment.

Yes, we live in the present moment, not in the past or the future. Your thoughts may wander back in time or you may be concerned about the future, but you must keep your focus on the present. Keep the slip in your hand and continue to ask yourself questions until you have complete clarity on the action you want to take with this. Cleaning, polishing, and preparing for restoration, or discarding it forever. Otherwise, learn from it and trade it for something useful.

Any slip that is no longer useful to you will be burned. Any slip you want to carry will be written on a new piece of paper that matches the colour of the new wall Karamchand is painting. Remember, the colour of your new wall represents your values and your purpose in life. Any artefact worthy of carrying will be cleaned and polished like the best happy memory before deciding where it will be kept. Go through each slip, one at a time, until you have dealt with each of them.

After you are done cleaning one room of your inner self, relax. Take a break, go for a walk, have a cup of tea, or stretch your body. After a brief pause, examine the second room of your inner self, followed by the third and fourth rooms of your inner self. Once completed, you are ready to celebrate the arrival of blessings, happiness, and success in your life.

Many things we keep are not for who we are but for who we wish we are. We make peace with our authentic selves by decluttering our fantasies. I agree that the process of getting rid of something can be challenging, especially if you have just-in-case clutter that includes the possibility that you will need it one day in the future. To enjoy the present, we must overcome our fear of the future. You have a beautiful mind that is aligned with your values and purpose in life. What better thing can happen to anyone than this alignment?

Declare 'I am beautifully aligned with my values, purpose, and inner self', believe in your creativity, and strengthen your relationships with friends, family, and neighbours.

Furthermore, it is natural to feel attached to your past. But this does not have to come at the expense of living in the present. Moreover, why shall you carry a past that is not beautiful and that does not help you live your present with peace? This brings you face-to-face with your attachments to your past, fantasies, and future. Work through the emotions associated with each and try to find more pieces in the present moment while still accepting yourself.

Decluttering your inner self is an ongoing process. However, it is rewarded with profound benefits that can significantly improve your quality of life. When you take control of interrupting, reframing, and challenging thoughts, you reduce their power over you.

Begin by identifying your core values. When your life priorities are clear, you do not waste time on things that will later cause you regret or cause mental suffering. When you set goals based on your values and priorities, you lay the groundwork for focused action and self-esteem, which keeps you energised. By being more in the present and being mindful, you can avoid many of the conflicts that arise during human interaction. This reduces mental distress and increases fulfilment. The less time you spend 'in your head,' the more time you will have to enjoy each present moment for the rest of your life.

GROW Strategy

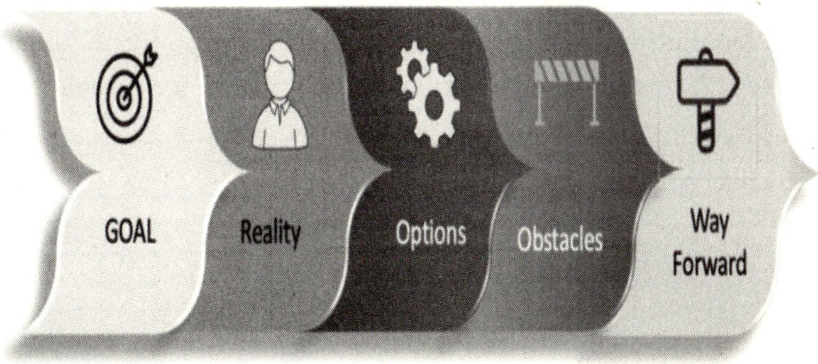

Chapter 7

Business Plan or Career Plan

So far, we have questioned ourselves and acknowledged our values. We now have a purpose statement and a growth plan. We learned time management, reflected on ourselves, decluttered our minds, and made an effort to upgrade our skills. All this contributes to building a strong personality. Now that we are all set in our personal career journeys, the time has come to take our professional side to new heights. Step one is to do a GROW analysis.

GROW model stands for:

G: Goal, what is it that we want to achieve?

R: Reality

O: Options

W: Way forward

Aligning our professional mission statement with our values is important for several reasons. When our values are reflected in our professional mission statement, it demonstrates that we are being true to who we are and what we believe. This authenticity helps to build trust and credibility with others because they can see that we are sincere in our work. In addition, we are more likely to feel motivated and engaged at work. When faced with obstacles or setbacks, this sense of purpose keeps us centred and committed to our objectives. As discussed in previous chapters, our values can serve as a guide for making decisions and organising our work. Our sense of purpose and well-being increases if we believe that our work is meaningful and has a positive effect. From that, we gain satisfaction and fulfilment.

A positive change comes when you take your professional side to new heights.

Sara had been a content writer for a while but felt stuck and uninspired in her line of work. She did not feel she was getting the respect she deserved, and her salary was stagnant. Therefore, Sara decided to pursue further education in graphics and web designing, which had always piqued her interest. She enrolled in an online course and put her skills through extensive study and practice. After completing the course, Sara applied for a web designer position at a leading tech company. Her portfolio and the skills she had learned through her additional education impressed the company. She received an offer with a pay raise compared to what she had been receiving.

With this new job opportunity, Sara's life started to change significantly. She had more financial stability. She was able to afford things that she had previously put off, like getting a car, going on vacation, and enrolling her 10-year-old child in a badminton academy that he wanted to join. Moreover, Sara experienced a renewed sense of purpose and motivation at work because she was eager to apply her new knowledge and skills. Sara's professional network expanded as she met new colleagues in her new job. She even started mentoring the younger designers, which made her feel happy and fulfilled. Sara's choice to advance her career opened up new doors for future success and growth.

Sara is not a fictional character. We have occasionally crossed paths and shared a few friends. Although we have not spoken in a while, we recently ran into each other at the Dubai Mall. In the brief meeting, I learned that Sara is now the owner of a web-designing business. She is supported by eight to ten employees. During our conversation, Sara mentioned that there is a GROW strategy behind her journey, from having a stagnant career to being a well-paid employee at an established company to becoming an entrepreneur and owning a small business.

Likewise, I have identified ways to expand my business using the same approach. Even though GROW is a famous strategy used by coaches for business and career growth, I have come across very few people who know about it. Here in this chapter, I will share my experience of running various workshops using this model.

Using the GROW model can help individuals clarify their goals, assess their current situation, explore new options, and develop a plan of action for achieving their desired outcomes. This can be a powerful tool for anyone who is involved in starting or growing a business, including entrepreneurs, small business owners, lenders, and even managers and employees.

There are four stages in the GROW model that provide a structured approach to setting and achieving career goals. By following these four stages, an individual gains clarity about their goals assesses their current situation, identifies potential obstacles, and develops a plan of action to achieve the desired outcome. In life, we are more dependent on available knowledge to improve our skills, and many times we fail to learn from experience. However, we cannot achieve satisfactory results unless we experience self-interference.

The GROW coaching approach emphasises the importance of self-awareness in achieving personal and professional growth. The model helps individuals to recognise and understand their strengths, weaknesses, and motivations before they can make meaningful progress toward their goals. GROW coaching approach emphasises the importance of a positive mindset and belief in one's ability to achieve their goals. It emphasises the importance of setting clear and specific goals and provides a structured framework for goal-setting.

Let us work on the plan for our professional development. In my experience, the GROW model is the best exercise. Let us therefore thoroughly comprehend the GROW model and its four stages.

G—Goal

Make sure your objective is clear, reasonable, doable, measurable and time-bound. The more specific your goal is, the more likely it is to be achieved. A smart goal increases the likelihood that it will be accomplished.

When we run the workshop with corporates often the goal is around the top line.

For example: A company's goal is usually to increase its overall sales. At times as a facilitator, it becomes important for me to ask open-ended questions like, by achieving this top line what impact can you see on the bottom line, that is in the net profit? You must be curious why such a question. Isn't it obvious that the bottom line improves when the top line is achieved? At times when our goals are too ambitious, we might lose sight of resources or overload the resources, like human resources or capital requirements. While making our goals, keep an eye on the resources because the bottom line is equally important.

Similarly, while this strategy is applied to individuals for their career goals, it is important to maintain the alignment of these goals with life purpose and values. One might set a goal so high that to learn the skill they have to sacrifice their family life. But what if, for that individual, family values are among the top priorities?

Have a check on the required alignment.

A friend of mine, Rahul, received a fantastic offer with a hundred per cent raise on his salary. To avail this opportunity he was required to shift to another country. I knew he could not live without his wife and his daughter. The family on the other hand was not willing to move to another country. What should he do? Go behind money or stay with the family? There is nothing right or wrong here. The only thing is that his decision must align with his life purpose and value.

On the other hand, Sam who was struggling to make ends meet and had the life purpose of providing the best for his family, chose to move to another country and to visit his family quarterly. His family was fine with his decision.

However, Rahul who was living a financially satisfactory life, chose to stay with the family as he was currently living the purpose of nurturing his family relations and giving back to society by educating a few kids from the nearby slum.

Once you have the goal aligned with the purpose and value of that company, we shall move to our next step which is R-reality.

R—Reality.

What is the reality of where I am and what I am doing today?

Reality is the current situation of a group or a person. It includes all the relevant events happening right now in your life, including the steps that you have already decided to take towards your goal. Analysing reality helps you explore any obstacles that may prevent your progress towards your goal. This involves taking an honest and objective look at the current situation, assessing the strengths, weaknesses, resources, constraints, and any external factors that might influence the progress.

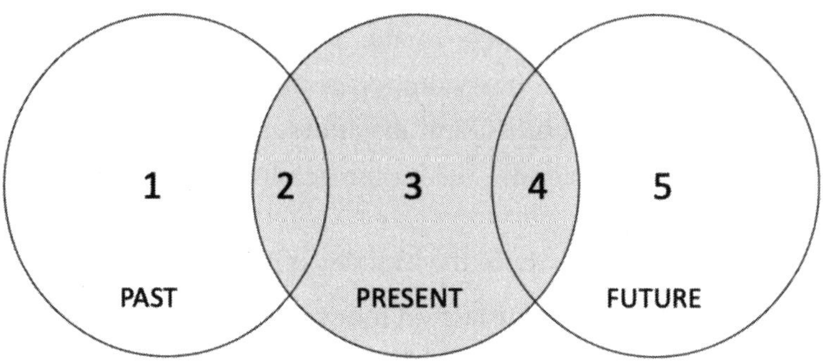

How we experience time.

By Rajesh Nagjee

Change is the only constant reality. Recently I learned a wonderful concept of temporality. So far we divide the time into three phases which are past, present and future. Mr Rajesh Nagjee developed a five-phase timeline.

- Past
- Past present
- Present
- Present future
- Future

Physically we all live in Phase 2 and Phase 4, mentally we can live in all five phases of the timeline. Our reality is Phase 2, in which I am living 'now' and 'now' already became a past when I wrote the word 'and.'

So, the question is what is the business or professional reality of Sam and Rahul?

Business reality refers to the actual state of affairs in the business world. It encompasses the practical aspects, challenges, opportunities, and dynamics that businesses face in their daily operations. The business reality often covers:

1. Product/service the business is providing
2. Customer satisfaction index
3. Employee satisfaction index
4. Shareholders satisfaction index
5. Access to CapEx
6. Core Team Alignment

7. Leadership skills
8. Positioning in the market

While our individual reality covers

1. Financial income
2. Family support
3. Skill sets
4. Financial savings
5. Growth mindset

Individual reality helps to identify our starting point and gain a realistic understanding of where we are, in relation to our desired goal.

O—Options

After evaluating their current reality, individuals can explore various options or strategies to bridge the gap between their current situation and the desired goal. This stage involves brainstorming ideas, considering different approaches, and generating potential solutions. By exploring a range of options, individuals can expand their perspectives and consider alternative paths to achieving their goals. After evaluating their current reality, individuals can explore various options or strategies to bridge the gap between their current situation and the desired goal. This stage involves brainstorming ideas, considering different approaches, and generating potential solutions. By exploring a range of options, individuals can expand their perspectives and consider alternative paths to achieving their goals.

For example:

For corporate:

Option - Add more products

Obstacle - Capital requirement

Option - Tap a new market

Obstacle - Human resource constraint

Option - Improve work culture

Obstacle - Limiting beliefs of management

Option - Infuse more capital

Obstacle - Winning the confidence of shareholders

Option - Core team on the profit and loss

Obstacle - Fear of risk in delegation

Option - Uplift the team skills

Obstacle - Team unwilling to spend time

The list of options and obstacles can keep growing, depending on the type of business and the team's size.

For an individual often I come across:

Option - Upgrade skills of qualification

Obstacle - Time and money

Option - Get a buy-in from the family

Obstacle - Unable to express and win fear of failure

Option - Develop a growth mindset

Obstacle - Inability to think beyond current responsibilities and requirements

I recall following all the instructions and carrying out all the exercises covered in earlier chapters. While I was working with those, the notion of 'money' kept popping into my head daily. Although it may not be the only important factor for happiness, money is necessary to meet basic needs and access opportunities and resources that promote personal development. Without the necessities of life—like food, shelter, and healthcare—it is challenging to concentrate on success or personal growth. For education-related travel and experiences, money is needed. It creates chances for entrepreneurship and career advancement.

Money is a necessity to accomplish everything one needs and wants in life.

With all of my plans, how do I expect to make more money, advance in my organisation, or earn more to meet my own and my family's needs?

Significance of money – One cannot possibly disagree with the significance of money and job satisfaction in life. A fair salary and benefits package help employees feel valued and secure in their jobs. Our overall well-being, including our physical and mental health, can be significantly impacted by it.

Significance of job satisfaction – When we are happy with our jobs or doing well in our businesses, we are more likely to feel good and have a sense of purpose, both of which are beneficial to mental health. Given that we spend a large portion of our lives at work, job satisfaction is crucial. We may be friendlier and more engaging to be around when we are content and feel fulfilled at work, which can enhance our relationships with friends and family. For personal fulfilment, work satisfaction is crucial. We are more likely to feel fulfilled by our work when we believe we are having a meaningful impact on the world.

The final step of the GROW model focuses on identifying the individual's commitment, motivation, and willpower to take action and pursue their chosen options. This stage involves evaluating the individual's level of determination, belief in their abilities, and willingness to overcome obstacles. It encourages individuals to develop an action plan, set milestones, and commit to taking concrete steps towards their goals.

While working on options and obstacles, you envision your way forward. Weighing our options with various pros and cons and evaluating them on the scale of facts and figures will assist us in reaching our next stage, which is the 'way forward.'

W—Way forward

It includes an action plan to help you move towards achieving your business or professional objective and to specify the deadlines. Winning over all the obstacles, pave the way forward.

Let us see corporate obstacles and a way to win over them.

Broadly these obstacles fall into three domains:

1. Capital related
2. Team related
3. Management related

So which do you think we shall take first?

If I were in your shoes, I would start by addressing management-related problems. Until we fix things at the top, nothing will really change. After that, I'd turn my attention to the team because making sure the team is working well together is just as crucial as having good management at the top. Once we have these two aspects sorted out, we can start looking at capital-related matters.

As management, either I can sit in my cabin and make that business plan or I can involve my team and give them ownership of the new business plan. Empower your team with delegation and authority and act as a coach to help them avoid the gaps. In a workshop, the most successful strategy is to have the core team own the profit and loss.

So, pick up each obstacle one by one, challenge them and win over them to have a clear way forward. Knowing our way forward paves the way for us to develop our professional mission statement and helps us to keep all of them in line with our values. Once you have developed an inclusive mindset, you will find ways to win over obstacles and find your way forward.

Yet, always have a backup plan.

Please note that as long as we are in the workshop, it will be acceptable to change our goals. Once we set our goals and decide the way forward, changing goals can only be our last resort in a dire situation.

Our methods may fail, and that is okay. We learn from our mistakes and failures and get better results after each trial. Thus, we should keep ourselves motivated until we achieve our goals.

Simply go through each stage of the GROW model. Think of the GROW model as a travel itinerary for the best way to conceptualise it. The framework includes targeted questions at each stage of the process that cover the key components. As a result, we first choose our destination, i.e., our goal. Before setting out on a journey, an objective must be determined. Goal refers to your aspirations and ambitions. Choosing where you want to be in life is the first thing you must do. Yes, keep in mind to think broadly.

Moreover, all these exercises discussed would mean nothing until we execute our decisions. In most organisations, goal planning and dreams fail because we do not execute them as we have planned. Therefore, in the next chapter, we will not only learn to design a vision but also an execution plan.

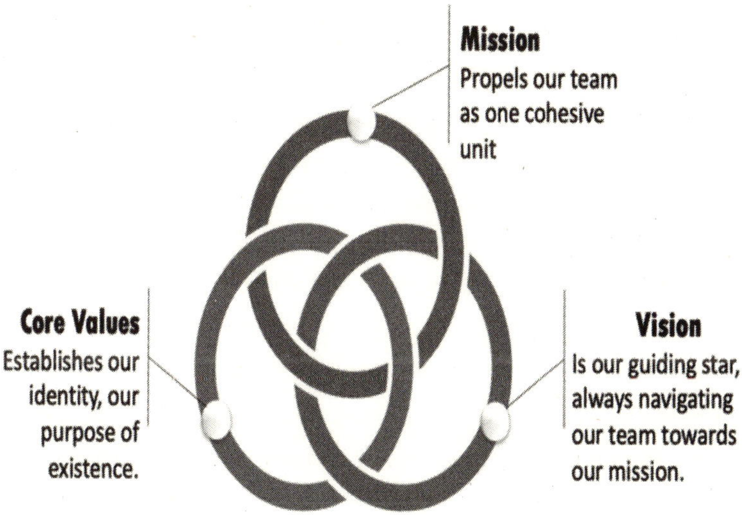

Chapter 8

YOUR MISSION AND VISION

'If you want to go fast, go alone. If you want to go far, go together.' When we speak about career or business growth, teamwork is an essential part of our plan.

It is a fact that no person possesses all the knowledge, skills, and expertise that are required to achieve success in any area. Therefore, teamwork is vital for career and business development and enables individuals to work together effectively towards a common goal. When there is a team, we need to keep them aligned and focused, and nothing can work better than having a mission and vision statement for the team.

For instance, if you own a readymade garment fabrication unit, it requires a team of individuals with different expertise and skills to work effectively together to produce high-quality fabric and garments. The garment factory hires a design team to create and develop new designs. Also, the design team works closely with the marketing team to ensure the designs are on trend and meet customer needs. Then we have a production team to manage the production process, which includes sourcing raw materials, cutting, and sewing the fabric. The production team makes sure that the products are produced to the desired specifications. There is a quality control team to ensure the quality of the fabric. They inspect the garments and fabrics at various stages of production and identify any defects or issues. The sales and marketing team is responsible for promoting the fabric produced by the factory. In addition, the cloth factory has a maintenance team that takes care of the equipment and machinery used in the production process and ensures that the machines are working in order. This team performs regular maintenance and repairs if required.

All the teams work effectively together to produce high-quality garments that meet customer needs and preferences. Every member plays a crucial role in ensuring the productivity and success of the factory, which are achieved through collaboration and communication between the team members. But do you believe all this coordination is possible if we don't have a mission and vision statement? In my experience, no.

Look at Nike's mission statement: 'To bring inspiration and innovation to every athlete in the world.' And Nike's vision statement is 'To do everything possible to expand human potential.'

A team combines people with various backgrounds and skills to work towards a common objective. Working together enables individuals to collaborate and share ideas, which leads to the development of innovative and new solutions. Being part of a team provides opportunities for individuals to gain knowledge, new skills, and experience from others and develop professionally. A team provides encouragement and support to overcome obstacles and stay motivated, which is crucial during challenging times.

The division of labour in a team enables greater efficiency and productivity. In addition, being a part of a team creates a sense of accountability as a team member, and in turn, they are responsible for each other's success.

When a team is united and working together towards

a mission, keeping the vision in focus, it leads to better communication, increased productivity, and a more positive work environment.

This is why, whenever I see team members struggling to achieve team spirit or direction or having formed tribes within the team, I use the workshop on 'Mission and Vision' to shift the energy to bring that new alignment and give them a purpose.

This workshop helps team members come out of their shells and look at bigger and better possibilities for the organisation as well as for themselves. It is as good as unleashing their willingness to work as a team. In addition, when we end this workshop, having a clear mission and vision serves as a foundation for teamwork. It assists team members in understanding their 'why' while working towards a common goal and supporting one another. When everyone is focused on a common goal, it will lead to increased team unity, productivity, and success.

Each time I deliver the workshop on 'Mission and Vision', the experience I receive is profound. I will share a case study and the steps to explain the why behind each part of this exercise.

A few years ago, an organisation in its 16th year of operation invited me to conduct a workshop. It had members working with them from the inception of the organisation, as well as fresh recruits.

For the workshop exercise, we created three flipcharts and placed slips of three different colours on each table.

After introducing myself, I started the conversation with the room by asking permission to invite each one of them in front of the room. Each member introduced themselves with their name, department, and how long they have been in the organisation.

After delivering their introduction, they were to give feedback on 'what is working well in the organisation and what is not.' Whenever we ask for feedback from anyone, it is better to set boundaries before we open Pandora's box.

Each member was asked to use two slips based on their tenure with the organisations:

More than 10 years,

More than 5 years, and

5 years or less.

Did you understand the 'why' behind this part?

Remember, everybody wants to be heard. However, often in an organisation the old, the senior people develop a sense of **perceived indifference**.

This perceived indifference may not necessarily be intentional. The reasons for perceived indifference may vary, but in my experience, often it is because of a lack of inclusivity, communication, and rapid changes. We can never deny the power of words, e.g., 'inclusivity.' How many stories does this single word tell you about an organisational culture? I can probably write another book on this title.

Whatever the reason may be behind perceived

indifference, as a leader of your organisation, it is our duty to keep employees motivated to maintain trust and commitment towards the organisation. Therefore, it is vital to approach the situation with an open mind to understand the root cause of the problem. It is important to hear every member and help them build a strong relationship with the organisation. When you allow someone to share, they feel heard, which is necessary for the employee to perform to the best of their abilities. Once you hear them and resolve their issues, you have a team which will perform to the best of their capability. Remember what Mahatma Gandhi said:

'The difference between what we do and what we are capable of doing would suffice to solve most of the world's problems.'

The question is, if so, why is it just one point? Why not hear them all? The reason behind this is that the workshop's running time is always constrained. Assume we start hearing ten slip notes per person. We will lose track of time.

Then what should we do if someone has multiple slips? The individual demands to be heard. To maintain order, and at the same time, respect the other person's space, it is better to say, 'Let me have just one more for the moment.'

When we ask them just for one, they will brainstorm and bring the one that covers most of their feedback.

Just keep in mind that we frequently have twenty or more things we want to say or do, but we are never sure where to start. In such cases, prioritising assists in deciding what to do first and determining what matters most at this particular time.

When you ask members to rank the importance of each statement, they will assess each one and then articulate the one perfect feedback that they could give. The activity is calming enough to clear the head.

I believe you comprehended the purpose of the exercise. Through this exercise, we gathered a lot of constructive feedback. Following that, I asked each table to discuss for five minutes and choose just the top two priorities or feedback that need to be addressed from the not-working segment.

From the ten tables in the room, I could only gather eight top-priority items, and you know why? Twelve other agendas picked up by tables overlapped. Just imagine the power of this exercise for a hundred-member team. We initially collected a hundred not-working agenda items. From that hundred agenda items, we filtered down to twenty top priorities, and from that twenty top priorities, we filtered down to eight unique top priorities.

Does life already feel easier for this organisation?

By the way, we are discussing what works and what does not work for the organisation. What is an organisation, though?

Any idea?

Let me help. An organisation is made up of all its members working together as a unit. Everything that constitutes a corporation is the collective effort of its members. Success or failure, positive or unsuitable, beneficial or toxic—it is everything that an organisation or its team members have accomplished collectively.

It is, now, time for some self-realisation for the team members, and this is the best part of this entire workshop. This exercise will shake the team members' consciousness, even if things do not come to paper. Here, each member is asked each team member is asked to take the second round towards the flipchart and come with two slips.

1. What am I proud of?
2. What am I sorry for?

Everyone has a deep-seated understanding of his or her accomplishments and regrets. In the next five minutes, everyone had to prepare two slips and come in front of the room to share and stick the slips on the flipcharts, but this time there were no different flipcharts for more than ten years, more than five years, and less than five years. This flipchart has just two sides. On the left half is, what I am proud of, and on the right side is, what I am sorry for.

Do you want to know the 'why,' or have you already understood the explanation given to the room?

We are all part of the organisation. Until we know what we are doing well and where we have made mistakes, there is no way forward. We will keep repeating what we are doing.

During the first exercise on what is not working, we got a clue as to which of our good acts are working negatively for the company and which of our good acts have a positive effect on the organisation.

Oh yes, we have used the term 'good' twice because of

my strong belief that no team member does something bad knowingly.

Both exercises, particularly the second, were intensive. Few team members went deep in their thought processes, while others stayed shallow. Even though some members were reserved and hesitant to share their good deeds that adversely impacted the organisation, what mattered to me was that they knew what they were doing incorrectly.

You would not believe it, but the energy in the room had shifted. It was more enlightened, and the atmosphere was no longer heavy. Each of them was already heard, could feel proud of what they had done, and could feel lighter by acknowledging their sorry. At this moment in the room, I felt like the cold breeze was flowing, and I could move on to the next part of this workshop.

What do you want to carry forward?

What do you want to leave behind?

Again, the same exercise, but now in a group of six, was conducted. The group decides what they want to carry forward and what they want to leave behind.

Once members are done with the exercise, we call one person from each group and put the note on the flip chart. Can you imagine a team that had chosen their future path in complete alignment with their team? What do you think will be discussed next? We know our way forward, but where are we heading? What is it that we want to accomplish, and is it the need of this organisation or just the want?

What do you think is the difference between need and want?

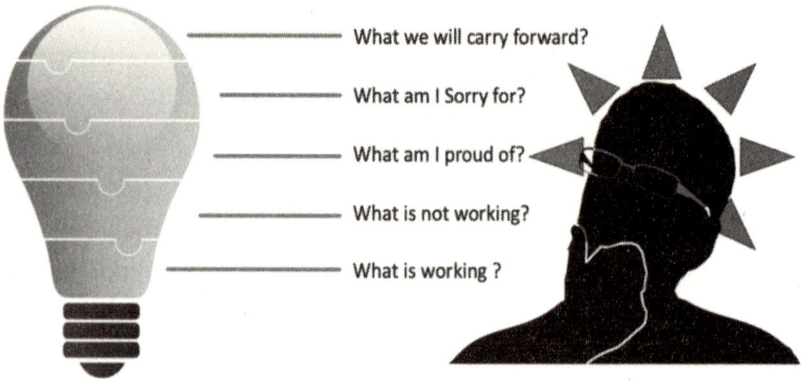

For example, a man wants a new car or a mobile phone because he likes the features and design. But if his current car or mobile phone is functional and meets his transportation or communication needs, he does not need a new car or a new mobile phone. Remember, nothing is right or wrong. In general, 'want' refers to the desire for something that is not essential. It is often a preference or a luxury that you can live without. While 'need' refers to something necessary for survival, well-being, or achieving a goal.

Nevertheless, who will define what is essential for me? For different people at different stages of their lives, the definition of a 'need' or 'want' may change due to factors such as personal preferences, culture, social status, etc. Nothing is right or wrong. Your right can be wrong from my perspective, and my wrong can be right from your perspective. However, what about the organisational perspective? The need or want of an organisation is better aligned with its organisational values.

Now the question arises:

What is the need or want for your organisation today?

See how wonderfully, through our exercises, we brought all the team's focus to the present.

Now divide the room into triads and ask them to prepare what is not a negotiable need in the organisation and what is a negotiable want. Make sure that this comes unanimously from the team.

Collect all the information you get from the room on the flip chart and read it out to the room. Ask the room if they wish to remove something. Ask them to highlight their top five needs and top five wants. Finally, ask the team to create the mission statement for the organisation.

What should you include in the mission statement of your organisation?

- **What** are we doing?
- For **whom** are we doing this?
- **Why** are we doing it?

Here are a few examples of two of the world's most renowned companies' mission statements.

Tesla: Accelerate world translation into sustainable energy.

LinkedIn: Connecting the world's professionals to make them more productive and successful

Our first success is aligning our team with our mission statement and getting to know the 'what', 'for whom,' and 'why' of our organisation.

Next, we need to decide **how** we are going to do that. This will be the vision statement. Again, what is the difference between a 'vision statement' and a 'mission statement?'

Someone once said to me, 'Mission is where I am going, and vision is how I am going to reach there.' In my experience, unless your vision statement is clear and achievable by measurement, it is challenging for the entire team to own it. Therefore, a vision statement should be simple, short, and clear enough, like a goal that can be measured.

A clear vision statement provides a shared understanding of the organisation's future goals and aspirations, which can help align employees, stakeholders, and partners towards a common purpose. Moreover, an achievable vision statement ensures that the organisation sets realistic and attainable goals that can be reached through its actions and strategies.

A vision statement that is too lofty or unrealistic can demotivate employees and stakeholders, as it may be seen as unattainable or irrelevant to the organisation's current state.

On the other hand, an achievable vision statement helps the organisation stay focused on its goals and ensures that the organisation's resources are used effectively and efficiently towards achieving those goals. A clear vision provides a sense of accomplishment and motivation for employees and stakeholders.

If I take the example of Tesla, where the mission statement is:

'To accelerate the world's transition to sustainable energy.'

The vision can be:

Vision 2025: One billion families in fifty countries living on sustainable energy.

So what is the mission and vision statement for your company? Remember that 'need, want,' and 'carrying forward' are the bases of mission and vision statements.

The cherry on top will be to define an action plan towards the vision, taking all the points of the 'Carry Forward' slide and covering all the 'needs' and 'wants' of your team and your organisation.

Do you know what you need to do in your organisation? If your answer is yes, do it before you get involved in something else.

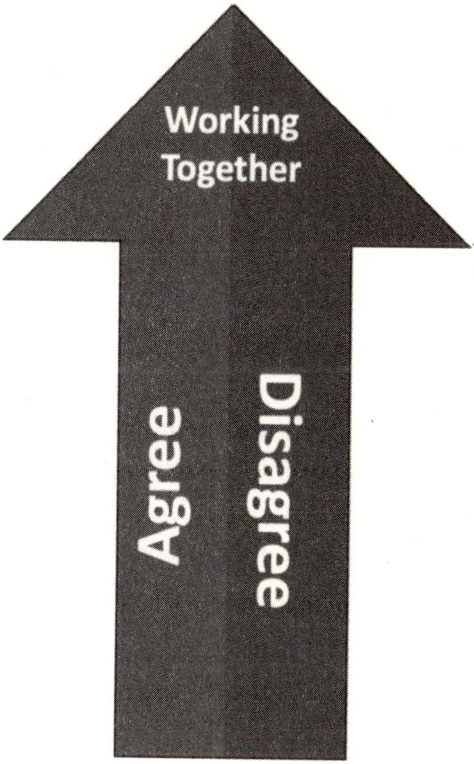

Chapter 9

The Growth Environment

I certainly believe that for growth, three things are essential:

First, knowing ourselves. It is the foundation upon which we build our achievements. We have gone through this knowing our value and purpose. We acknowledged why we are doing what we are doing. We believe in ourselves and align our values with our purpose and mission. We cultivate self-discipline and prioritise our actions to maintain our focus and energy towards achieving our goals.

The second is our people. Whether it is our business or our career, we work in teams. We have aligned with our team and designed our mission and vision. Our team is willing to take on the challenges and is ready to act without burning out. This is their own mission, and, we as leaders, are all in to provide them with the required resources and support.

The third is the environment in which we work.

There is a saying, 'Environment is stronger than will.'

Your environment shapes you. It inspires and motivates you to push beyond your limits, motivates you to learn new skills and take on new challenges. A positive environment fosters a culture of continuous learning, collaboration, and innovation.

So what is your growth environment?

I have read a lot on the subject from various writers, especially John Maxwell. Recently, I attended a session in Dubai where John extensively spoke on the importance of a growth environment for creating personal and organisational success.

Maxwell has also written a book, *The 15 Invaluable*

Laws of Growth, in which he asserts that growth thrives in favourable conditions. If we want to experience personal growth, we must assess our surroundings and make changes that support our growth objectives.

Your surroundings have an impact on everything you do. Up to half of your success is determined by the people, occurrences, and data sources surrounding you. It might inspire you to keep going and help you grow. Another possibility is that you may be inundated with criticism, which might stop you from developing.

As a human being, you evolve through interaction with everyone around you. This is what John Maxwell has to say about it.

> If we want to experience personal growth, we must assess our surroundings and make changes that support our growth objectives. The people we hang out with, the places we go, the things we surround ourselves with, and the media we consume—all of these things have an influence on what is happening inside of us, and growth will only occur when we welcome it.

Often I ask this question to my team members, 'Where do you spend most of your active hours?'

I spend most of my active hours in my office.

So what should the environment of my office be to keep me encouraged?

For me, the most important things are:

1. A neat and clean environment – Decluttering my desk, my drawers, and my mind is a regular activity for me.

When our surroundings are organised and clean, it helps us focus on our work. A cluttered living area or workspace can be distracting. It hinders our ability to concentrate.

For instance, you have a desk job and are responsible for multiple projects. Your files are scattered around your desk, making it difficult to locate important documents. This results in wasted time searching for the document, missed deadlines, confusion, and stress. On the other hand, when files are organised in a systematic way, such as using colour coding or labelled folders, locating files becomes easy.

A clean environment makes a positive first impression on others. It shows that you are organised and responsible, which helps build trust and respect with others.

2. A well-defined role – For me, it is very important to know my Key Performance Indicators and have enough work to do during my office hours.

'An empty mind is the devil's home.' When a person's mind is not occupied with constructive thoughts, it becomes a breeding ground for negative thoughts or behaviours that prove harmful to his and his team's growth. I want my team to acknowledge their duties. They should neither be overwhelmed with the work nor be hunting flies or burning their time on social media. A team should have a clear understanding of what is expected of them in terms of responsibilities, rules, and performance standards. This can be achieved through job descriptions, performance metrics, and regular communication. A well-defined role should provide individuals with opportunities to learn and develop. This also includes training programmes, mentorship, technology, job shadowing, equipment, and access to industry events.

A well-defined work environment fosters a supportive and collaborative culture. This can be achieved through team-building activities, recognition programmes, and open communication channels.

3. Agree to disagree work environment – Have you heard about the concept 'Agree to Disagree'? Great workplace cultures rely on the concept that everyone has the right to express their opinion.

Agree to disagree is a concept that suggests that it is possible for two people to hold opposing views on a topic but still respect each other's opinions and work together productively.

An 'agree to disagree' work environment can help prevent conflicts and promote a more harmonious work place culture. Therefore, I prefer a growth environment where my teams are not afraid to express their ideas or objections.

A company calls the meeting to discuss the issues. To reach the best solution, every team player should contribute to the discussion according to their ability. Allowing the expression of ideas helps uncover the rational thoughts driven by an individual's point of view. When a team member is given a role in a discussion or meeting, it enhances innovation because the team focuses on developing ideas and solutions.

So, how do you put agreeing to disagree into practice at work?

- Respectful Communication: Promoting respectful communication can help foster a workplace culture in which opposing viewpoints are valued and discussed constructively. Active listening, acknowledging each other's points of view, and avoiding personal attacks or insults are all examples of this.
- Compromise: It is sometimes possible to find a middle ground that satisfies both parties, even if they do not fully agree on each other's points of view.
- Focus on Common Goals: Reminding everyone of common goals and objectives can help in refocusing discussions and keeping disagreements from becoming personal or distracting.
- Recognise Differences: Recognising that it is natural for people to have different perspectives and opinions can aid in the creation of a workplace culture in which opposing viewpoints are accepted and valued.
- Progress Forward: The ultimate goal of 'agreeing to disagree' is to move forward and continue

productively working together, even if there are differences of opinion. This can be accomplished by seeking common ground or agreeing to respect each other's opposing viewpoints.

One common piece of advice for personal and professional growth is to step out of your comfort zone. As it is said, 'The sky has no limit.' Then, why limit ourselves? Why should we stay in our comfort zone? To grow, take risks, try new things, and face your fears.

4. **Challenging Environment: An environment that challenges me to get better** – I would like an environment where I have opportunities to grow. New opportunities that challenge me but do not break me

Getting out of your comfort zone can be challenging, as it often involves facing uncertainty and potential failure. Nevertheless, it can also lead to new experiences, opportunities, and perspectives. As it is said, 'Sitting in the best room does not mean you are sitting in the right room.' To promote growth and evolution in both an individual and an organisation, it is critical to constantly challenge oneself. The only way to innovate is to put the outdated models to the test. An organisation must constantly challenge itself to stay driven, pursue novel endeavours, optimise stability, and get ahead of its counterparts. However, take a calculated risk.

Identify areas where you feel comfortable taking small risks, and gradually increase the level of risk as you become more comfortable. Stepping out of your comfort zone and facing new challenges does not always have to be a huge leap. Small steps can lead to big growth over time. In addition, it is important to play in your strength zone. Introduce yourself to new and diverse opportunities. Challenge yourself to explore uncharted domains, but in a setting that encourages you to hone your strengths. Nevertheless, before taking on a challenge, accurately assess your skills, knowledge, and capabilities.

5. **Nurturing Leaders** – Next on my list is the growth environment that nurtures. An environment that not only encourages leaders but also raises other leaders.

Yes, at every level of organisation, nurturing is the way of management. A successful leader can motivate the team and increase productivity. Identifying employees with leadership potential and assisting them in developing their skills and behaviours yields significant benefits for both the employees and the company. A productive leader provides others with a space to learn, develop, and change. Keep in mind that the people you are nurturing are likely to fall or make mistakes. However, the acquired environment provides the necessary resources and support for the individual to hone his leadership qualities. Therefore, a growth environment should foster a culture of teamwork and collaboration by promoting the sharing of knowledge and encouraging teamwork and communication.

6. **Promote a growth mindset** – Provide constructive feedback that is actionable, specific, and timely. In addition,

recognising and rewarding individuals who demonstrate leadership qualities such as creativity, initiative, and problem-solving skills area crucial part of nurturing leaders. Nursing leadership and trust go hand in hand. Trust is an essential ingredient for effective leadership, and leaders who are trusted are more likely to be effective. The foundation of effective teamwork is confidence.

7. **An environment of trust** – Before talking about trust, I would like to express my gratitude to Mr Stephen R. Covey for his book *Speed of Trust.*

In his book, Covey argued that trust is the foundation of all successful relationships, including those in the workplace. He believed that trust is essential for effective leadership and that leaders who build trust with their team are more likely to be successful.

Trust, according to Covey, is built through a combination of character and competence. Characteristics such as integrity, honesty, and authenticity are examples of character, whereas skills, knowledge, and expertise are examples of competence. Covey also emphasised the significance of communication in the development of trust. He believed that clear, honest, and frequent communication is necessary for developing trust with others.

If you want employees at your workplace to not feel like cogs in a machine, ensure that the work environment is full of trust. Showing trust in your employees is the fastest, easiest, and most successful way to boost their performance.

8. An environment full of gratitude – Gratitude towards God, vendors, and our team members build a healthy workplace.

Humans are social beings, and most of our relationships are based on reciprocity. Our deepest relationships are driven by gratitude. Practising gratitude at work fosters compassion and consideration among colleagues. Gratitude goes a step further than appreciation. It is about seeing the complete picture. Gratitude is about taking the good with the bad so as to accurately assess the situation and be thankful for the kindness of people around you.

Thus, do not take things for granted and create an environment where the employees want to come and work. Create an environment where people feel secure enough to give their best.

9. An environment of security – Unless people feel secure, they cannot give their best.

Security should be a top priority when working in a factory or an office. While employees are working on their shifts, their possessions and personal information must be kept secure. A workplace that prioritises privacy and security protects sensitive information from unauthorised access or

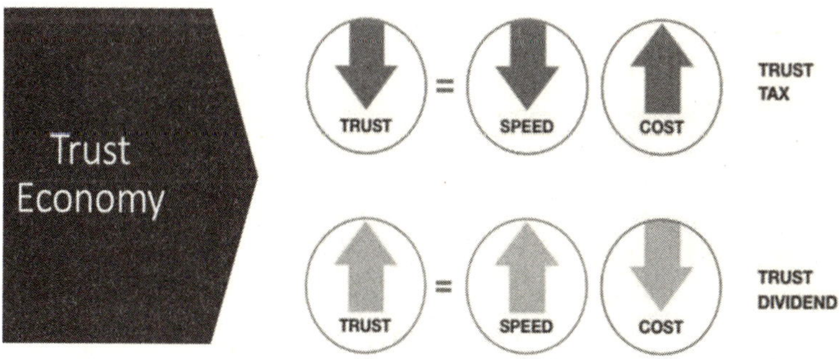

disclosure, such as trade secrets, financial data, and personal employee information. Employees are more likely to trust their employer and feel confident in their work environment when they know their personal and professional information is kept confidential and secure. This results in higher job satisfaction and retention.

10. A sense of belonging is the feeling of being valued, accepted, and included in the workplace. Employees with a strong sense of belonging feel like they are part of a team. Their contributions are recognised, and they can be themselves without fear of being judged. Furthermore, a sense of belonging promotes diversity and inclusion in the workplace by cultivating a culture of respect for and acceptance of diverse perspectives and backgrounds.

Employers can promote a sense of belonging in the workplace by creating a culture of inclusion and providing opportunities for team-building and social events. Recognise and celebrate employee accomplishments. Provide a supportive work environment where failure is not feared.

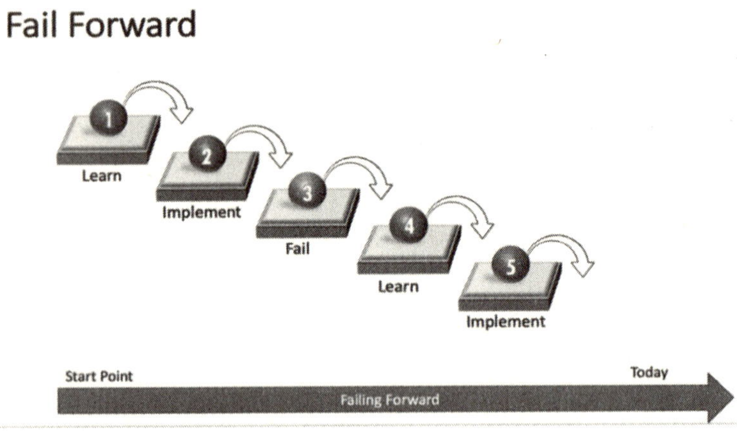

Have you heard Mumbai residents talk about their city? They say *Amchi* Mumbai means My Mumbai.

Similarly, the people of Jaipur invite visitors to their city by saying *Padharo Mhare Desh*, which means Come to my country or city. This is a feeling of belonging.

Similarly, I need to feel ownership and a sense of relevance in the workplace. Just ask yourself honestly. Will you wear a

T-shirt or a jacket with your company logo while on vacation? Imagine that level of belonging where the company and I are not two different entities.

11. An environment where failure is not fearful – The fear of failure affects performance.

If the employees are scared of sharing their ideas, the company's work culture may be in jeopardy. It is the responsibility of the leader to promote fairness in your organisation. A few steps to get started to encourage a fearless work environment include:

- Do not react negatively to news of any kind. Instead, think of ways to improve the situation.
- Avoid misunderstandings by making your intentions known. Clearly explain what you are trying to accomplish and why.
- Before accepting or rejecting any idea, acknowledge it. This will increase comfort and confidence among the team members.
- Recognise that failure is a natural part of the learning process, and create a culture where it is okay to make mistakes. Encourage employees to share their failures and the lessons they learned from them.
- Offer support and resources to help employees overcome challenges and learn from their mistakes.
- Celebrate big and small successes to recognise and reward progress and hard work.

12. A forward-thinking work environment that emphasises growth and progress – I want a work environment where what is next is always on the employees' list.

People are forward-focused. As John Maxwell claims, 'Reflection is an important component of growth. However, the purpose of reflection is not to dwell on the past. Rather, it is to gain insight into the future. We move in the direction we are facing, so we can only take a step forward into growth if we are not worried about what we could have done differently.' Organisations that look to the future and consider how to transform it inspire their employees to grow.

Last but not least on my list is the growth environment, where success is celebrated.

13. An environment of fun and appreciation

Are you giving your team's accomplishments the attention they deserve? Is it second nature for you to celebrate success?

Celebrating accomplishments can boost confidence and motivation. Appreciation can also help your organisation's reputation, retention, and attraction of top talent.

Activities that promote socialisation and teamwork among team members, such as team games, may be included in celebrations. A company may choose to honour a team member who has contributed to the organisation by allowing them to lead a group of colleagues in an hour-long celebration that includes snacks and drinks. Celebrating successes at work is essential for uniting a company culture and instilling a sense of belonging and connection with others in the workplace community. Increased success celebrations at work may lead to increased productivity. This is because employees may believe that the organisation values and requires them.

The celebration recognises completed work and expresses gratitude to those who perform it. Remember to honour habits and qualities as well as numbers. It does not take much effort, but it means a lot to people. It is a party. So have some fun!

When we nurture a growth environment, the entire organisation and its employees grow. Such organisations are bonded together to face any market challenge or take up any impossible project and make it possible.

Chapter 10

FOCUS AND ACCOUNTABILITY

The secret behind successful people is developing certain habits that help them to be positive and productive. The most important success mantra for achieving more in life is focus and accountability.

My grandmother used to tell me stories from the Mahabharata. Sage Dronacharya once challenged the Kauravas, Pandavas, and other students to aim at the eye of a fish. The fish was swinging from a branch of a tall tree, going round and round. All of the students attempted to hit the target, but only Arjun's target struck the fish's eye. Guru Dronacharya asked students, one by one, what they saw before aiming. Some said they saw a tree branch. Others said they could see a fish and still others said they could see the fish's mouth. When Guru Dronacharya asked Arjuna the same question, he replied that he could only see the eye of the fish and nothing else. This is the extreme of focus, and the question is, how close can we go in today's life to this kind of focus?

We are human beings living in this materialistic world, getting distracted by a variety of opportunities to fulfil the materialistic dream. The important thing is our awareness that we have moved away from our focus and our attempt to bring it back. I learned this concept during my experience with Vipassana. Every now and then, most of us lose our focus during mediation and feel as if we are failing.

In the workshop, I heard Mr Goenka explain the wandering nature of our thoughts. Being human, it is normal to lose our focus, and the art we need to practise is to become aware and bring it back. There is no need to feel guilty or feel like a failure. Lose it, bring it back, lose it, bring it back, and you will notice that your focus improves every time.

True individual strength and effectiveness come from keeping a check on your focus and bringing it back into alignment with the primary objective of your life. When our attention wanders from one thing to the next, we lose our focus, which results in slow progress towards our mission.

Focus is essential for success because it allows you to direct your energy and resources towards achieving your objectives. Your performance in a range of areas, such as academic, athletic, and professional endeavours, is enhanced by being focused. Focus allows you to pay attention to details, make better decisions, and produce better results. It boosts creativity by allowing you to experiment with new ideas. When you concentrate, you produce more in less time. You can complete your work more efficiently and effectively if you minimise distractions and stay on task.

Consider a student who wishes to excel academically but is unable to concentrate and may check their phones, browse social media, or engage in other activities unrelated to their studies. As a result, they may miss important deadlines, underperform on exams, and struggle to meet their academic objectives.

If the student is focused, on the other hand, they can prioritise their studies, stay on track with their assignments, and devote their energy to learning and understanding the material. This can help them get better grades, understand the subject better, and position themselves for future success.

Therefore, focus is an essential component of success in any field. You can make progress towards your desired outcomes and reach your full potential by staying focused on your goals and avoiding distractions.

Whether you are trying to finish a report at work or run a marathon, your ability to focus can mean the difference between success and failure. The ability to focus on something in your surroundings and direct mental effort towards it is crucial for acquiring fresh knowledge, achieving goals, and performing well in a variety of circumstances.

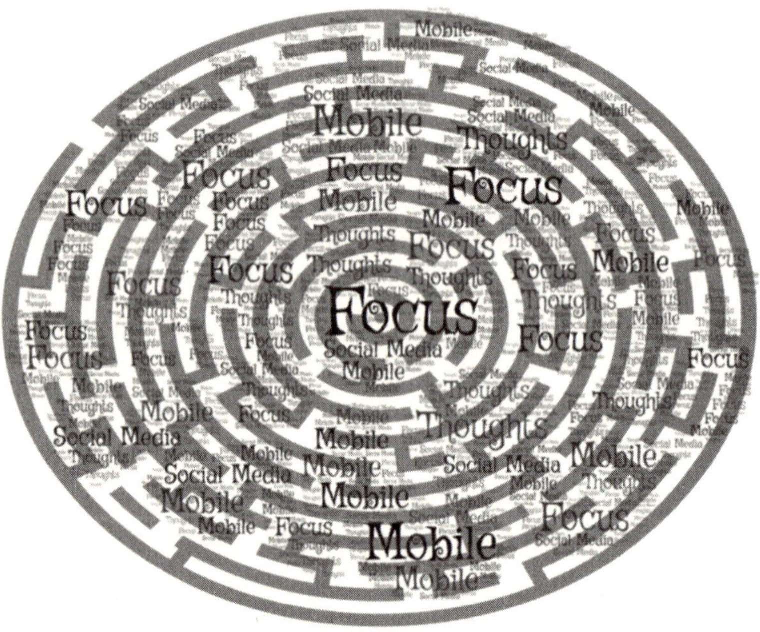

We are living in the age of knowledge. We have an abundance of information available to us at all times. It is easy to become disoriented in the never-ending stream of news, emails, and social media updates. In addition, when people try to do multiple things at once, their focus and productivity suffer. It is easy to beside-tracked by random tasks or distractions when you don't have a clear plan or schedule.

Being more mentally focused is, thankfully, attainable. The more you work on improving your focus, the stronger it becomes. However, it will necessitate considerable effort on your part.

Is there a way we can manage our thoughts?

Have you ever been on a treadmill at a speed of twelve and an incline of six? Did you ever get distracted by that high speed and incline?

No thought ever comes to our minds while we are busy with a focus on maintaining our balance and speed and pushing ourselves to keep up with the running belt underneath our feet.

What is that which happened on the treadmill that is not happening on a normal day? It's worth giving it a thought and exploring your own answers. For me, it was the awareness that if I don't focus, I will get injured. I knew how important it was to remain focused, and I could.

Will you feel emotionally injured if you are not able to achieve your goals or indulge in activities far away from the purpose of your life or career?

Very recently, I attended a session where the importance

of making a to-do list was discussed as a tool for managing our focus. How do we prioritise tasks on our desks? Often, we end up procrastinating on some tasks for various reasons. It might be because of a lack of skill, complications involved, or focus required, and this causes us to think about this work off and on and lose our focus.

One of the important reasons for losing our focus is the frog syndrome. Do not worry. You are not suffering from a disease. The frog simply means the most important and toughest thing you have on your desk.

For instance, if we have a task to accomplish that we are not comfortable with or are not sure how to accomplish it, in order to maintain focus, we need to follow the 'Eat the Frog' strategy. Eat the Frog says to work on the frog first, which means finishing the toughest task on your desk, and the rest of the job will be fun. By completing the toughest task on your desk, you would earn more energy to complete other tasks at hand rather than drain energy and lose focus thinking about the frog which is the toughest task.

By tackling the most challenging task first, you are less likely to procrastinate and put it off until later in the day or week. This approach helps you avoid the stress and anxiety that often come with procrastination, which can drain your energy and negatively affect your productivity.

Let's get into the details of how the Eat the Frog strategy helps:

- Completing a difficult task first thing in the morning gives you a sense of accomplishment and builds momentum for the rest of your day. You may feel more energised and motivated to tackle other tasks on your to-do list, leading to increased productivity.
- Reducing Stress: When you complete your most challenging task first, you may feel a sense of relief and reduced stress. This can help you feel more in control of your workload and reduce the likelihood of feeling overwhelmed.
- Increasing Focus: By focusing on one task at a time, you may be able to maintain greater focus and avoid distractions. This can help you work more efficiently and effectively.

- Prioritising Important Tasks: By identifying and completing your most important task first, you ensure that it receives the attention it deserves. This can help you avoid the trap of constantly working on lower-priority tasks and neglecting important projects or goals.

If you are unsure how to implement the 'Eat the Frog' method, we have a few tips for you.

- Plan and identify the most important task(s) the night before.
- Break the task into smaller, more manageable steps.
- Set a specific time to complete the task and hold yourself accountable.
- Focus on the benefits of completing the task, such as a sense of accomplishment or reduced stress.
- Celebrate your progress and reward yourself for completing the task.

What if you have two frogs, that is, two difficult tasks, on your desk? Which one will you pick first?

Maybe the phrase stated by Brian Tracy will help.

'Your frog should be the most difficult and largest item on your to-do list,' says Brian Tracy.

The most difficult aspect of any important task, however, is getting started on it in the first place. When you begin working on a valuable task, you will be naturally motivated to continue. I would like to emphasise the significance of another phrase here, 'Eat the elephant bite by bite.'

In the words of Desmond Tutu, 'There is only one way to eat an elephant, and that is one bite at a time.' By this, he meant that any task is possible if completed gradually, one step at a time. It is an adage which means that trying to bite off more than you can chew is often a recipe for disaster. As a result, rather than attempting to eat the entire elephant in one gulp, cut the elephant into pieces and focus on taking one bite at a time. We tend to worry too much about the problem rather than taking the necessary steps to solve it. Remember that worrying never solves future problems. It only takes away the peace and time we have right now. Simplify your life. If you have a large task on your desk, take a moment to reflect, plan, and then act. The proverb, Eat an elephant one bite at a time, applies to any problem. This method allows you to focus and concentrate on one step of the problem at a time, which results in a better outcome. The best part is that you can share the elephant pieces with your colleagues, i.e., delegate the task if required, so that you can focus on what is important.

Writing my first book was like the elephant-sized frog on my desk. This task has been on my vision board for many years, and I was just procrastinating it every day. Recently, I met the publisher of this book, Anshu, at a BNI global conference in Singapore, where I discussed with her my desire to write a book, and she promised to assist me. I discovered some light at the end of the tunnel, but I had to walk through it.

After returning from Singapore and avoiding contact with her for several months, we finally spoke, and she assisted me in cutting the elephant into pieces.

'Pankaj, if you are unsure about what all matters to include in your book, can you, for a start, just write the ten topics for the ten chapters of your book?' said Anshu.

This was incredible. I accomplished it in just one day. In just one day, I prepared ten topics on which I wanted to shed light on and shared them with her. Anshu, then, served me the second piece of the elephant, instructing me to write ten pages for the first chapter. I gained confidence and energy after finishing the ten pages. The completion of the first chapter convinced me that I could complete the task of writing this book. Today, as I write the tenth chapter, I must thank Anshu for making it possible for me.

I have not only shared my knowledge with you all by writing this book, but I have also acknowledged that if I can write a book in thirty days, anyone can accomplish the most difficult task on their desk by cutting the biggest giant into pieces. The only thing you need to learn is how to manage your focus and hold yourself accountable.

Accountability

What goes hand in hand with focus is accountability. We can be focused but not accomplish the desired milestone on time. To stay on time, it is important to stay accountable.

The concept of an accountability partner was introduced to me around seven years ago, and ever since, I feel this is one of the most important nuggets I have earned during my peer-to-peer learning.

Before I finish the book, I would like to talk about accountability partners and the role they play in your success. An accountability partner is someone with whom you collaborate to hold each other accountable to a specific goal or set of goals. This person could be a friend, family member, colleague, or even a coach or mentor. As an example, in my case, my wife, Shalie, is and will always be my accountability partner.

It is not necessary for you to travel alone. Having someone to assist us on our journey can be a fantastic motivator. It can aid in removing behavioural creases and serve as a motivator if you start to lose focus.

The purpose of having an accountability partner is to foster mutual support and encouragement, as well as to hold each other accountable for progress towards your goals.

According to studies, having an accountability partner increases your chances of success by ninety-five per cent. Accountability is about discovering oneself. It is about mental training to develop habits that lead to success and growth. It entails being accountable to oneself and others for one's actions and working with steady mindfulness. Accountability is a philosophy in which we strive to instill optimism and good thoughts and reactions in everything we do.

Accountability partners can be beneficial in a variety of ways:

- Provide motivation and encouragement when you are feeling discouraged or unmotivated.
- Hold you accountable for keeping your promises and sticking to your plan.
- Provide a new perspective and new ideas for achieving your objectives.
- Celebrate your accomplishments with you and assist you in seeing your progress.

When looking for an accountability partner, look for someone trustworthy, dependable, and supportive. You should also be clear about your goals and expectations and set up a regular check-in schedule to review progress and discuss any challenges or roadblocks you may be encountering.

How would you pick someone who would play such a significant role in your life? A partner for accountability is someone you are willing to honour with the authority to question your progress. Someone who will keep a check on your progress at regular intervals. Choosing the right accountability partner is a critical step in reaching your objectives.

Here are some pointers to help you find the right person:

1. Look for someone who shares your goals or interests. It will be easier to hold each other accountable if you are pursuing similar goals.
2. Find a dependable accountability partner. Your accountability partner should be someone you can rely on to show up and follow through on commitments. They should be responsible, dependable, and have a track record of achieving their own objectives.
3. Find a supportive person. Choose someone who is upbeat and encouraging and who will encourage you even when times are tough. Avoid negative or critical people because they can be demotivating and counterproductive.
4. Find someone who is accessible. Make certain that your accountability partner has the time and availability to commit to regular check-ins and follow-ups. It may be difficult to maintain consistent accountability if they have a busy schedule or conflicting commitments.
5. Think about working with a professional accountability partner, such as a coach or mentor, if you have a specific goal or area of focus. These individuals are skilled at assisting others in achieving their objectives and can provide personalised support and guidance.

Finding someone you trust, respect, and feel comfortable working with is the most important factor in selecting an accountability partner. Spend time getting to know potential partners and determining whether they are a good fit for your needs and goals.

Finally, consider how you will get there if you need to achieve a goal in twelve months. How do we set the parameters to determine our success?

Every one of us started out as students and worked our way up to become graduates. How did you get to the graduation?

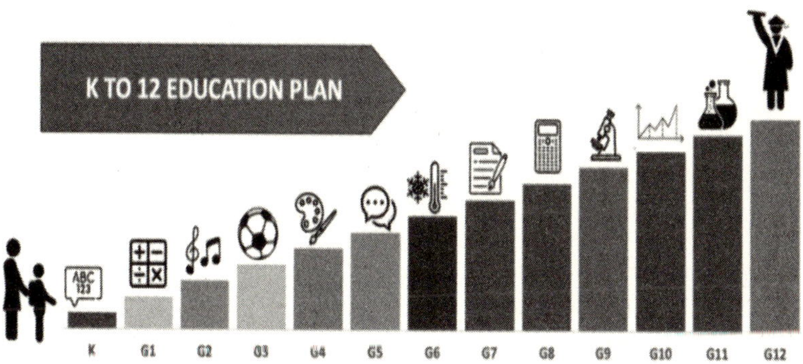

There was a daily schedule to follow. There was a curriculum to adhere to and there was a quarterly assessment. I have heard there are now weekly assessments. Then, there was a final exam, after which we were promoted to the next grade.

Most of us have been living this way for fifteen to twenty years, and yet we want to know how to achieve the goals we have in our lives. We just need to delve deeper into our journey and fill the gaps with experiences and lessons.

So, what is the first step you are going to take now?